A
READING
CENTURY

STUART HYLTON

Sutton Publishing

First published in 1999 by
Sutton Publishing Limited · Phoenix Mill
Thrupp · Stroud · Gloucestershire · GL5 2BU

British Library Cataloguing in Publication Data

A catalogue record for this book is available from the British Library.

ISBN 0-7509-1996-5

Title page photograph: Part of the University College campus on London Road.

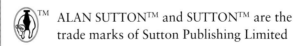 ALAN SUTTON™ and SUTTON™ are the trade marks of Sutton Publishing Limited

Typeset in 10/13 pt Sabon.
Typesetting and origination by
Sutton Publishing Limited.
Printed in Great Britain by
The Bath Press, Bath, Avon.

CONTENTS

INTRODUCTION AND ACKNOWLEDGEMENTS 1

1900 A New Century 2

1903 Trams 8

1911 Greater Reading 12

1914 War 19

1916 The Somme 27

1918 Armistice 33

1926 The General Strike 39

1934 Famine and Fascism 46

1939 Goodbye Trams, Hello Mr Hitler 56

1947 Freeze and Floods 61

1961 Kool Kats, Black Sheep and The Palace 67

1968 Multi-Racial Reading 70

1971 Rock and Roll – Here to Stay? 79

1974 Bulbs – Suttons Go West 87

1977 Biscuits – Huntley & Palmers Stop Baking 91

1978 Civic Pride 96

1980 Beer – Bridge Street Brewery Closes 100

1987 The Great Storm 103

1988 Glory Days at Elm Park 106

1990 Poll Tax and the Canal 110

1999 and Beyond – The Future for Reading 118

2000 Whatever Next? 123

INDEX 124

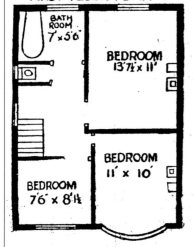
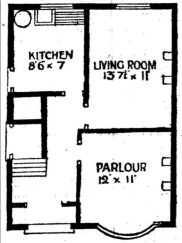

INTRODUCTION AND ACKNOWLEDGEMENTS

When I first wrote about the history of Reading, back in 1992, there were relatively few books about the subject. I am happy to say that this shortage has now been remedied, and it seems that scarcely a month goes by without some new corner of the town's history being uncovered. There is sometimes a tendency to think that Reading's history ends with the growth of beer, biscuits and bulbs as the town's staple industries, but the town has also witnessed momentous changes more recently. Now that the century is drawing to a close, it is an opportune moment to look at the whole story of twentieth-century Reading.

I have used the same approach as in my last two Reading books, looking at events as they were reported in the local newspapers, and using contemporary photographs and advertisements to add to the period flavour. There was far too much material for me to cover, so I had to be selective. I have included items of purely local importance, such as the introduction of the electric trams to Reading in 1903 or the great floods of 1947, as well as national events that had a dramatic impact on the people of Reading, such as the two world wars. I also looked at some of the lesser stories being reported in the local newspapers, in order to give a flavour of what everyday life was like for the people in different parts of twentieth-century Reading. The one thing I can be sure of is that everyone will disagree with something from my choice of newsworthy events!

Partly to avoid duplication (but mostly in a cynical attempt to get you to buy my other books, *Reading at War* and *Reading: the 1950s*), I have made no reference in this book to the second world war or the 1950s. Further fascinating information on these periods is available from all good booksellers.

A note on my main source of material: we are used to talking about the *Reading Chronicle*, although a previous generation would have known it as the *Berkshire Chronicle*. But at the beginning of the century people were reading something called the *Berkshire Chronicle, Windsor Herald and General Advertiser for the counties of Bucks, Oxon, Hants, Surrey, Middlesex and Wiltshire*. Once they had printed that lot on the masthead, it was surprising that they had any space left for the news. For the sake of simplicity, I will just refer to the *Chronicle* throughout.

Margaret Smith and her colleagues at Reading Central Library were, as ever, very supportive during the researching of this book. They are now part of Reading Borough Council, who are co-sponsors of the book, along

(Opposite) *1933 – the Kent Wood Estate goes on the market*

1

with the *Reading Chronicle*. The *Chronicle* allowed me to use their photographic records of the latter part of the century. Some of the photographs I used were acquired for a previous book from local collectors, and I am particularly indebted to Graham Parlour, Richard Reed and John Griffin. John Painter gave me the benefit of his wide knowledge of Reading in commenting on a first draft of the text and Sally Swift helped in linking the publication of the book to the rest of the Borough Council's millennium celebrations.

Needless to say, any outrageous views expressed in this book are entirely my own, and not those of its co-sponsors or of anyone else involved in its production.

1900

A NEW CENTURY

Our century begins at the height of the Boer War. A lynch mob roams the streets of Reading, looking for Boer sympathisers, and Tilehurst decides that it is against street lighting.

As the people of Reading entered the new century, most of the news on the pages of the local newspaper came from abroad. For this was the height of the Boer War, and the thoughts of many Reading people were with their sons and husbands, fighting in distant South Africa. There were detailed accounts of the campaign – Winston Churchill's escape from the clutches of the Boers was major news, Mafeking was besieged and Ladysmith was about to be relieved, giving rise to a string of tasteless jokes. The opening weeks of the century saw four Berkshire men killed and seventeen wounded in fighting at Colesburg.

Letters home from local men were given great prominence in the *Chronicle*. They were no Wilfred Owens, but the straightforwardness of their accounts seemed only to heighten their impact. One guardsman wrote: 'The Boers could not hit us much while we were on the ground, but the moment we commenced to rush, the bullets rained . . . the Scots Guards very soon retired on our right, but our Captain told us we were Grenadiers and could not retire, so we still advanced and got to within about 500 yards from the enemy's trenches when the ammunition ran out and we could do nothing but lie flat on the ground and our captain would not retire.'

'Our Captain told us we were Grenadiers and could not retire'

Sergeant Henry Hudson wrote: 'The Boers are great cowards. If they are hard-pressed, they hoist white flags and put on hospital crosses to protect themselves, and if our fellows stop firing to receive the flag they shoot our fellows down, but we have now got used to their little games.'

Sapper Adcock of the Royal Engineers told a sorry tale: 'About eight o' clock some officers of the Army Medical Corps came along and, to my surprise, asked for volunteers to bury the dead. . . . Well, the first grave we dug was about thirty foot long and three foot deep, and we put 53 Scotchmen into it, 34 of the Black Watch alone. Every man of us was crying, some so loudly that you could hardly hear the minister.'

In Reading, the conflict fired the patriotism of the local people. When the troops at Ladysmith were relieved, the bells of St Lawrence's Church were rung and flags were flown from public buildings and private houses alike. In the evening, crowds of people paraded through the streets, carrying flaming torches and Union Jacks, and a meeting at the Town Hall was interrupted by the people outside singing the national anthem and 'Rule Britannia'.

Patriotism also had its darker side. For example, rumours began to circulate that a meeting of the South African Reconciliation Committee was taking place somewhere in the town. This organisation existed to promote a peaceful settlement and to 'disseminate accurate information' about the war – or to act as a pro-Boer pressure group that 'made traitorous speeches', depending on whose point of view you took.

A mob, which eventually grew to an estimated thousand people, had no doubt which point of view they took, and they went rampaging round the town centre, looking for the meeting. Acting upon information received, they descended upon the Foresters' Assembly Rooms in Bridge Street. Those who could pack into the building searched it from top to bottom, while the remainder stood outside, singing 'The Soldiers of the Queen' in a lusty and no doubt terrifying manner. Finding no trace of the guilty parties, the mob moved on to the Cross Street Hall, where a member of the Hearts of Oak Society was addressing an audience on the fascinating subject of superannuation. The mob, by now led by a group of soldiers, burst into the hall, and it took a while to persuade them that superannuation was not some kind of devilish Boer plot. Eventually, having tried other venues and tiring of their unsuccessful search, the mob dispersed. It turned out later that the meeting had been held in a private house.

The conflict even affected those too young to take part in it, in one case with tragic consequences: 'Considerable sensation was aroused in the west end of Reading on Sunday afternoon by the report that a lad, named Sidney Herbert Richardson, had been shot in the eye by a playmate, and had been taken to the Royal Berkshire Hospital in an unconscious state.' He had been among a group of boys playing Boers versus English, and fifteen-year-old Walter Grant had for some reason been playing the game with a loaded pistol. Richardson died an hour or two after entering hospital and Grant, who had been a close friend of the deceased, 'appeared to feel his position acutely' when he was arrested and charged with manslaughter.

MIRACLE CURES

Life in Reading, however, was not totally preoccupied with the war. The patent medicine advertisers, untroubled by the pettyfogging rules of any Advertising Standards Authority, vied with one another to see who could make the most outrageous claims for their products. Who among us did not suffer from something that they could cure?

Dr Scott's Pills . . . are certain in their curative effects of the following ailments in both sexes or children – Bilious and liver complaints,

1903 – the wonderful world of Edwardian patent medicines with pills for famous females

indigestion, wind, spasms, foul breath, nervous depression, irritability, lassitude, loss of appetite, dyspepsia, heartburn, sour eructations, lowness of spirits with sensation of fullness at the pit of the stomach, giddiness, dizziness of the eyes, habitual costiveness and all those other symptoms which none but a sufferer can describe.

I for one have never had any trouble with sour eructations or habitual costiveness since taking them; as for my symptoms, which none but a sufferer can describe, they have cleared up entirely. For those readers of the female persuasion, the advertisers were a little more coy about the curative effects of their products: 'Towles' Pennyroyal and Steel Pills for females quickly correct all irregularities, remove all obstructions and relieve the depressing symptoms so prevalent with the sex.' If all else failed, 'Noads Powders are excellent in cracked legs, swollen heels, hidebound, loss of appetite, etc. . . . They increase the strength, invigorate the spirit, assist digestion. They are the best alterative to give at any time, as they purge the blood from all gross humours and bring the animal into splendid condition.' Unfortunately, these were prescribed for horses. My own preference is for a medication that carried the following ringing endorsements: 'It is peculiarly well-adapted for medicinal purposes' (*The Lancet*) and 'It is evidently of high quality' (*British Medical Journal*). Odd publications, you might think, in which to find recommendations for Kinahan's Whiskey.

STREET FANTASY FOOTBALL

On the football field, Reading triumphed 3–0 against Bristol Rovers in January 1900. They played in the Southern League at this time, against teams as obscure as Thames Ironworks and Sheppey United, and others who later achieved Premier League status, such as Southampton, Queen's Park Rangers and some outfit called Tottenham Hotspur. Some would-be Reading players found their training interrupted as the courts cracked down on football matches being played in the streets of the town, such as

1909 – Milward's footer boots, for Edwardians wishing to score.

Erleigh Road and Whitley Street. A five shilling fine was commonplace. Footballers trying to play in these streets today would not survive much beyond the kick-off.

MOTORING MADNESS

Most of the traffic in those days was, of course, horse-drawn. In April 1900 the Automobile Club of Great Britain launched a 1000-mile trial of motor vehicles, with the object of advancing the automobile movement in the United Kingdom. Some eighty-four cars took place, in what must have been one of the biggest assemblies of horseless carriages ever seen in the country up to that time. The aim was 'to prove that the best of these vehicles is capable of covering long distances and mounting steep hills'. The route of the trial came through Reading: 'When the cars reached Reading, a large number of people were on the lookout at the Cemetery, and others lined the route all along London Road, Southampton Street, Bridge Street, Castle Hill and the Bath Road up to the boundary, whilst a few cyclists and pedestrians found their way to the entrance to Calcot Park, where the motor carists partook of breakfast as the guests of Mr Alfred Harmsworth.* . . . The motorists were all covered in dust and were for the most part clad in thick coats, with peaked caps and a pair of uncoloured glass goggles with leather dustproof flaps, which gave them the appearance of an uncouth-looking highwayman of the olden days.'

*Alfred Harmsworth, later Lord Northcliffe, the newspaper magnate and sponsor of the trial.

OUTDOOR RELIEF – AND HEALTHY EXERCISE

People who were down on their luck had no Welfare State to fall back on. Instead there was Parish Relief. The Reading Board of Guardians reported a worrying increase in the numbers seeking outdoor relief in 1900: 279, compared with 212 for the corresponding week the previous year. On the bright side, the numbers of lunatics in asylums were down from 151 to 139. Welfare from the Guardians generally had to be worked for unless you were severely disabled. A tramp named John Smith got seven days' hard labour for neglecting his task of breaking stones while an inmate of the workhouse – despite the not unreasonable defence that he could not stand up.

SPECIAL EDUCATION NEEDS

The education authorities were equally robust in their methods for dealing with those who failed the system. They announced plans to build an extra classroom at the Oxford Road School to house those pupils covered by the Elementary Education (Defective and Epileptic Children) Act 1899. Their surveys of the school population of Reading had found around sixteen children who were, in their view, unfit to be educated at an ordinary school. Politically correct terms like 'special educational needs', 'people with disabilities' and 'challenging behaviour' did not feature greatly in the description of their clients in those days: 'Some of them were bordering on idiocy, others were physically deformed so as to make them quite unsuitable to be placed with other children; some were an intolerable nuisance to the schools where they were, and although the expense [the Education Department was] put to would be considerable . . . it would be a great relief to the teachers to be rid of these children.'

According to a 1912 survey, one Reading family in five lived in serious poverty.

Other surveys of the Reading school population revealed further worrying statistics. For example, 40 per cent of the children were found to have defective eyesight. A high proportion of schoolchildren (20 per cent of the pupils at the Central Boys' School, and 12 per cent of those at Newtown, for example) were found to be putting in a substantial working week in addition to attending school. Some were working up to thirty or forty hours a week for as little as one shilling. Children who were doing three or four hours' work before arriving at school not surprisingly found it difficult to concentrate on their lessons.

TILEHURST RESIDENTS KEPT IN THE DARK

In Tilehurst, much of which was outside Reading's boundaries at the time, a public meeting was held to discuss the possibility of lighting some of the streets by gas. Walking into the village from the railway station or from the stile in Norcot Road was at that time a hazardous activity, illuminated only by the 'parish lantern' (to wit, the moon). It was a journey that lone women were often unwilling to undertake. The authorities had considered oil lamps and even the new-fangled electricity, but finally proposed gas on grounds of cost. The proposal suffered the same fate as many such improvement schemes put forward in Reading throughout the previous century. The so-called Economisers rejected the expenditure, arguing that people should provide their own lanterns. The meeting closed and 'parishioners were left to grope their way home in the dark as best they could'. Their opposition

Prospect Park, bought in 1901 for the benefit of the Reading public.

was later confirmed in a poll and the *Chronicle* attacked this decision in an editorial. The paper's attitude to the development of Tilehurst is in marked contrast to the resistance to building so often seen a century later: 'The village's situation is healthy and there could be no obstacle to the rapid growth of the village as a residential neighbourhood, if the people would only realise the necessity of providing some of these modern improvements, which naturally intending residents demand.'

But in another matter, the paper was very much on the side of the Economisers. Reading had had a horse-drawn tramway service since 1879 but lack of investment had left it in a poor condition. The Council proposed promoting a Reading Tramways Bill in the next Parliament, with a view to taking over the service and putting in electric trams. In an editorial headed 'Reading Ratepayers Beware!', the paper warned that the scheme could cost them £200,000 or more: 'This is a policy which we have condemned and shall continue to condemn. It is the kind of policy which has in the past landed the town into the extravagant expenditure on the sewerage scheme, the sewage farm and the lowering of the Kennet, and the result will be the same in this case. It is the duty of the Town Council to take the ratepayers into their confidence before committing them to such an enormous expenditure and this they have not done. . . . We notice that our radical friends have advocated not just the Tramways Bill, but the purchase of the Electric Lighting Company, the incorporation of Caversham and other extravagant and expensive schemes. . . . the Borough debt already amounts to over £650,000. What will it be if all these extravagant schemes "in the air" are carried out and what will the rates be?'

They would shortly find out.

1903

TRAMS

The death of Queen Victoria has ushered in the Edwardian age. Reading Council replaces its horse-drawn trams with the new electric variety and Reading Football Club introduces a ban on spectators shouting horrible things at the players and officials. The local police introduce the first primitive speed traps for motorists.

The *Chronicle*'s initial lack of enthusiasm for the Corporation's electric trams had entirely vanished by 22 July 1903, when the service was officially opened: 'Wednesday was a red letter day in the history of Reading, for the electric tramway system, the completion of which has been so eagerly awaited and desired, was at last a *fait accompli* and the mayoress switched on the current at the generating station and declared the tramways open. . . . There is no town in England which can surpass Reading for the excellence of its tramway system, either as regards the construction of the permanent way, the character of the generating plant or the arrangements which have been made for the convenience of the travelling public.'

The celebrations began with a grand luncheon at the Town Hall, attended by the great and the good of the Borough and visiting dignitaries from London and elsewhere. George Palmer, biscuit tycoon and the town's Member of Parliament, started it off with a toast: 'Success to the Reading Corporation Tramways undertaking.' A good deal more toasting and celebrating went on, and it was 3.45 in the afternoon before the dignitaries made their more or less steady way across to the generating station at Mill Lane for the official opening. The mayoress turned on the current to begin a procession of ten trams, with the lead car driven by the Mayor, Alderman Bull.

Moving slowly at first, because of the huge crowds congregated around the depot, the line of red-and-cream trams made their way up to Broad Street. Once on to the Oxford Road the crowds thinned out and the trams were able to reach the dizzying speed of 16 miles per hour. At the Oxford Road railway bridge there was a bit of a squeeze, as the trolley buses' poles were only just able to go under without touching the heads of the passengers. (They actually had to lower the level of the roadway under the Caversham Road railway bridge to fit the trams through – the pavement there is still a lot higher than the road, even today.)

1903 – Buffalo Bill rides the range down the Oxford Road.

TWO DAYS ONLY.

READING, FRIDAY & SATURDAY, JUNE 26 & 27.

GROUNDS - OXFORD ROAD, *opposite Pulsometer Works.*

BUFFALO BILL'S WILD WEST

Congress of Rough Riders of the World

Headed and Personally Introduced by

COL. W. F. CODY

(BUFFALO BILL)

NOW TOURING THE PROVINCES.

Visiting the Principal Cities and Greater Railway Centres Only

4 Special Trains, **500** Horses, **800** People,

THE ENTIRE GRAND PROGRAMME

Will positively be presented undivided and uncurtailed

TWICE DAILY, RAIN OR SHINE

A Pre-eminent Exhibition of Universal Interest.

The One Grand Ruler of the Amusement Realm

A veritable Kindergarten of

History-teaching facts ; not

on fiction founded.

LIVING OBJECT LESSONS

Taken from the pages of realism and illustrated by the very men who have assisted in making familiar the most famed of the World's Mounted Warriors. A gathering of extraordinary consequence to fittingly illustrate all that has and can be endured by Virile Martial Manhood. Cowboys, Cuban Patriots, Mexican Ruralies, Bedouin Arabs, South American Gauchos, United States Cavalry, Russian Cossacks, American Artillery, Western Girls, Roosevelt's Rough Riders, Royal English Lancers, and all the features that made the Wild West famous.

100 AMERICAN INDIANS

Genuine "Blanket" Red Men, Chiefs, Warriors, Squaws, and Papooses from the Uncappappa, Brule, Ogallalla, Arapahoe, Cheyenne, Yankton, and Sioux Tribes. New and interesting arrangement of the well-known

WILD WEST INCIDENTS

Introducing the Pioneers of the Plains, who tell the story of the progress in the Great Drama of Civilization by

Pictures of Border Life.

The Stage Coach "Hold-up," Cowboys' "Round-up," Riding Wild-Bucking Bronchos, Indian War Dance, Attack on the Emigrant Train, Equestrian Feats and Skill, Warlike Pageants and Military Exercises.

Interesting Scenic Episode of the Spanish-American War,

Being a Realistic Military Spectacle of the

BATTLE of SAN JUAN HILL.

The Vast Arena Illuminated at Night by Two Special Electric Light Plants.

Two Performances Every Week Day. Afternoons at 2. Evenings at 8. Doors Open at 1 and 7 p.m. One Ticket Admits to all Advertised Attractions.

PRICES OF ADMISSION—1s., 2s., 3s., 4s. ; Box Seats, 5s. and 7s. 6d. Children under 10 years half-price to all except the 1s. seats. All seats are numbered except those at 1s. and 2s. No Tickets under 4s. sold in advance. Tickets at all prices on sale on the grounds at hours of opening, and tickets at 4s., 5s., and 7s. 6d., on sale at 9 a.m. the day of exhibition at

HICKIE & HICKIE'S, PIANO & ORGAN MERCHANTS, 100, BROAD STREET.

A FREE ENTERTAINMENT FOR EVERYBODY

Visiting the Exhibition Grounds at 11 a.m., Preliminary Open Air Concert by the Famous Cowboy Military Band and other interesting features.

Will Exhibit at OXFORD JUNE 25. SWINDON, JUNE 29.   2482

The trams took their distinguished passengers (many of whom, no doubt, did not make a habit of travelling on public transport) to the Oxford Road terminus and then back to the eastern end of the track at Wokingham Road, before depositing them in Broad Street in time for those who had come from London to catch the 5.03 train back to Paddington. Once the dignitaries had finished playing, it was the public's turn to have a go. The scenes were described as being like Coronation night, but without such boisterous behaviour, as large crowds of people struggled to get on board. The trams seated forty-eight people on their two decks but overcrowding restrictions were ignored in the effort to ensure that as many people as possible experienced the new wonder of the age. The brilliant electric illumination of the vehicles was particularly striking as the evening drew on.

The Coronation procession of King Edward VII in King's Road, 9 August 1902.

The construction of the electric tramway had not been without its difficulties. In addition to the initial opposition of the newspaper and other Economisers, the private tramway company tried to challenge the legality of the Council's right to buy them out. Simonds' Brewery also opposed the building of the generating station, which was sited opposite their brewery in Mill Lane, on the banks of the River Kennet.

As its name suggested, a mill had stood on this site since the days of William the Conqueror. The construction of the generating station entailed building over, or filling in, parts of the old millstream and another watercourse called Gunter's Brook (after Nicholas Gunter, a Mayor of Reading in the days of Queen Elizabeth I). Simonds were concerned that these developments would make their brewery more prone to flooding and would make it more difficult to load their goods on and off canal barges.

Crowds gather at Broad Street and Mill Lane to witness the opening of the electric tram service in May 1903.

Ministers of churches along the route were worried that the noise of the trams would disturb their devotions and so, for these parts of the track, the rails had to be mounted on wooden or lava blocks instead of the usual granite setts. There had been negotiations with the local authorities in Caversham

The northern terminus of the tramway – the Caversham Bridge Hotel. Caversham Council would not meet the cost of extending it north of the river.

The new tramway under construction. This is the Broad Street/West Street junction.

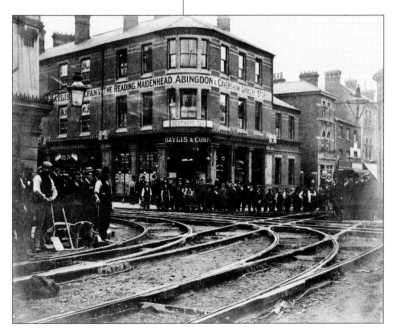

(then a separate local authority) about extending the tramways into their area. Caversham Urban District Council had been keen on the idea until they realised that it would entail widening Berry's Corner, just north of Caversham Bridge, at their own expense. Thus it was that the north/south tram route terminated at Caversham Bridge. Last but not least had been the need to maintain public transport for the people of Reading during the upheaval of constructing the new tramway. The old horse-trams had been running right up to the Tuesday before the opening ceremony and the new track had itself been tested with horse-drawn trams before the power was turned on for opening day.

The Council had ambitious plans for the tramway. They pitched the fares at a very low level (including a one penny workmen's return ticket) to try to maximise patronage. They planned to run 900,000 miles worth of trips each year – the equivalent of 12 miles for every man, woman and child in the Borough. The trams were to serve the town until almost the outbreak of the Second World War, when trolley buses and motor buses replaced them.

To say that the *Chronicle* covered the opening fully is an

understatement. Pedants from the Borough Surveyor's Department were brought in specially to itemise the minutest detail of the new service. Imagine the joyful scenes around Edwardian breakfast tables, as father read extracts from the report and the children tried to guess the diameter of the chimney at the generating station, the chemical composition of the steel used to construct the rails and their weight per yard, not to mention the name of the manufacturer of the nuts and bolts that held the rails together. Even the letters page contained a call for the new trams to be free from advertising. (There was little likelihood of this call being heeded, though, as it brought in an estimated £1,000 a year to the Council.)

The first week of operating the trams proved highly successful. On the first Saturday alone, they carried over 32,000 passengers and took the grand sum of £139 15s 10d in fares. The extent to which the *Chronicle* had been converted to the cause can be seen from this unsolicited puff for them in its columns: ' "Why go out of Reading for a holiday, when you can get unlimited fresh air on an electric car?" might be an attractive advertisement for the electric cars. Certainly their usefulness in this direction cannot be exaggerated, and the numbers who use them for this purpose alone, especially during the evening, show what a boon the Corporation have provided for the townspeople and supplies quite a new attraction for visitors to Reading.'

Perhaps inevitably, the week of the opening also featured the first prosecution of a small boy (one Frederick Lambourne, aged twelve), for placing a stone on the tram tracks, to see what effect the tram wheels would have on it.

Not everybody was overjoyed at the arrival of the trams. The fact that the rails were set anything up to three inches below the level of the road, and that the authorities went around splashing water over the tracks to keep them clean, made them a serious hazard to cyclists. Reports came in of eight accidents in a single afternoon, and cyclists were in danger of falling under the wheels of an oncoming tram.

'Why go out of Reading for a holiday, when you can get unlimited fresh air on an electric car?'

SPEAK KINDLY TO THE REF

But amid all the excitement about the trams, there was just room in the paper for some other news. On the letters page, the National Association for the Suppression of Bad Language was looking for people to sign their pledge to abstain from lewd and defamatory language. Since their foundation, they had gathered many notable patrons, including the Archbishop of Canterbury. We may safely assume that Elm Park was not a hotbed of recruitment for them, since this letter appeared in the paper at about the same time:

Dear Sir,

I am desired by my Directors to ask you to give publicity in your next issue to the following extracts from notices posted at Elm Park Football Ground:

1. The Police have special instructions to eject from the ground any persons using objectionable language regarding the referee, linesmen or players;

2. All clubs are required to prevent the use of objectionable language by spectators. In the case of a breach of this rule, any spectator may be removed from any ground, and such force used as may be necessary for the purposes of effecting same.

These rules will be strictly enforced and any spectators ejected from the ground will be debarred from future admission.

H. Matthews – Secretary

Their concern is not surprising. At a time when illegitimacy carried a far greater stigma than it does today, cries of 'Who's that person in the black whose parents are not married?' could be deeply wounding to a referee.

SPEED FIENDS OF READING

Pioneer motorists were also starting to come to the attention of the police. An early version of a speed trap was set up on the Bath Road at Sulhamstead. A measured half-mile was marked out and a constable concealed in a ditch with fieldglasses and a stopwatch. His efforts were rewarded by the detention of a Member of Parliament, no less: a Mr C.D. Rose, who queried the accuracy of this method of assessing speed but was none the less fined £5 with 9s 6d costs for doing an alleged 26mph. Also caught were the chauffeur of the Hon. C.S. Rolls (soon to form his historic partnership with Henry Royce) and a Mr Harry Hampshire from Slough, a speed-crazed demon who was pulled up for doing 8mph on his motorcycle combination! In one case, at least, the evidence was unambiguous. A chauffeur was arrested for doing 50mph in a racing car owned by his employer, and which – even in 1903 – was capable of 90mph.

There was some sympathy for the motorist in the editorial columns, prompting this early example of the convicted motorist's whinge 'Why aren't you out catching criminals?' (which seems unfair, since you never hear of serial killers asking the police why they aren't out arresting motorists): 'Putting aside the fact that it is infinitely easier to catch a motorist than a burglar, the obvious platitude must be faced that no person can be in two places at once and, if a constable has orders from his superior officers to perch for hours in a lonely hedge, like some ungainly wild fowl, or to secrete himself in a disused drain, after the manner of a loathsome reptile, upon the chance of snaring some motorist, who is doing no harm to him or anyone else, it is clear that he cannot, at the same time, be keeping a vigilant eye upon property and protecting the public – which, by the ignorant, has generally been supposed to be his chief duty.'

Do I detect an editor who has just collected a speeding ticket?

Mr Harry Hampshire from Slough, a speed-crazed demon who was pulled up for doing 8mph on his motorcycle combination!

1911

GREATER READING

The Titanic *prepares for her maiden voyage and George V has succeeded Edward VII. Reading expands its boundaries north of the river, over the metaphorical dead bodies of some Caversham residents. Suffragettes demonstrate in London and the first British airship is wrecked. Reading, too, is terrorised by suffragettes and balloonists.*

Reading had had a substantial boundary extension shortly before the century began. The town more than doubled its size in 1887, taking in

Whitley and parts of Tilehurst. Much of this was related to new laws setting up sanitary authorities to provide decent sewerage. In urban areas like Reading, this responsibility fell to the local authority. In the surrounding rural areas, it was the job of the Poor Law Guardians, who were less well equipped to carry out major capital works. But if they wanted the urban fringes of Reading which they administered to be plugged into Reading's sewers, the price was the incorporation of those areas into the Borough. The new battle for the incorporation of Caversham and the outer parts of Tilehurst into Reading was waged for several years until its resolution in 1911.

Caversham was described as being merely a village in the 1880s, but in the years that followed it grew rapidly to become a sizeable suburb of Reading. Up to 1888 there had not even been any democratically elected local government there, apart from the Poor Law Guardians. However, by the 1900s Caversham had its own Urban District Council although many key services – such as the police, roads and education – were still run by the County Council, based at Oxford, some 28 miles away.

The strength of the link between Caversham and Reading was undeniable. Almost half of the working population of Caversham was employed in Reading, and many of their children were educated in the Borough, in particular at the Swansea Road School. The people of Caversham already benefited from many of the local authority services in Reading, such as the trams, the library, museum and art gallery, the parks and pleasure gardens, not to mention the water supply. Joining with

Church Street, Caversham, just before its incorporation into Reading in 1911.

Reading would give them access to new facilities, such as the Park Fever Hospital (which would have been particularly useful, given the epidemic of scarlet fever that had swept through lower Caversham in 1908). Even those services which Caversham Urban District Council did provide were often inferior to those of their neighbours. Their sewage works was creaking from having to cope with a rapidly growing population. They were the poor relations of the Henley Poor Law Guardians; the workhouse was based some miles away, in Henley itself, and Caversham paid a third of its costs but received only a sixth of the benefits that were distributed among the needy.

Caversham schooling was inferior to Reading's; their teachers were worse paid, scholarships few and far between and the school leaving age was thirteen, compared with fourteen in Reading. (This last point actually led a number of families to move from Reading to Caversham, so that they could get their offspring out of school and earning their keep a year earlier.)

Standards of animal husbandry were so low north of the river that Councillor John Rabson condemned Caversham as being a health hazard to Reading. The one benefit of living in Caversham appeared to be that you could be interred in Caversham cemetery for a lower price than that charged to outsiders. This privilege was retained after incorporation, giving any anti-incorporation residents of Caversham at least something to look forward to.

For despite all the arguments in favour of incorporation, there were still those in Caversham who opposed it. Even as the legislation was going through Parliament, the Leader of the Urban District Council, Mr H.C. Dryland, was calling for 'no surrender'. The arguments of the anti-incorporators are difficult to make out, ninety years later. The lower rates and other taxes in Caversham were a central plank of their case, yet Reading's exposure of the inadequacy of their services led them to promise all sorts of improvements (waterworks, road improvements, investment in the fire brigade, their own hospital for infectious diseases and even a boundary extension into Mapledurham) that would soon have swallowed up any savings. Among their other arguments was the view that Reading had not consulted its own residents about the boundary extension. (This was true; in fact a number of Reading people, including a former mayor, thought they would be better off without taking on this liability north of the river.) There were also claims that Reading had not fulfilled its promises to the areas that it had taken in at the last boundary extension.

November 1911 – Reading filmgoers are promised film of Scott's trip to the South Pole. Scott did not get there until January 1912 and by March he was dead.

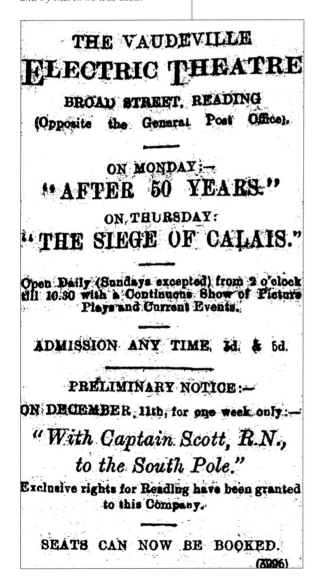

THE VAUDEVILLE
ELECTRIC THEATRE
BROAD STREET, READING
(Opposite the General Post Office).

—

ON MONDAY :—
"AFTER 50 YEARS."
ON THURSDAY :
"THE SIEGE OF CALAIS."

Open Daily (Sundays excepted) from 2 o'clock till 10.30 with a Continuous Show of Picture Plays and Current Events.

ADMISSION ANY TIME, 3d. & 5d.

—

PRELIMINARY NOTICE :—
ON DECEMBER 11th, for one week only :—
"With Captain Scott, R.N., to the South Pole."
Exclusive rights for Reading have been granted to this Company.

SEATS CAN NOW BE BOOKED.
(3996)

Last, and quite possibly least, was the complaint that Reading Borough Council's accounts were not audited by the Local Government Board, but by three elective auditors. One of these, a shocked Mr Dryland pointed out, 'was a Socialist and has no professional qualifications whatsoever'. Mr Dryland was supported by an association of Caversham property owners, which had been formed to fight the incorporation. One of the last to hold out in opposition was the Crawshay family, the owners of the great estate at Caversham Park. Their property was eventually excluded from the 1911 boundary review on the grounds that the estate would certainly never be built on. It did not become part of Reading until 1977, by which time it was better known as Caversham Park Village, and was most definitely part of the built-up area. But all the opposition was futile. As the *Chronicle* put it in 1911: 'Incorporation is going inexorably forward and it is time that those ardent but mistaken opponents of the scheme on the Caversham side of the water bow to the inevitable and save the trouble and expense of a prolonged fight in the Houses of Parliament.'

So Caversham became a part of Reading in 1911. Some of the outer areas of Tilehurst became part of the Borough at the same time, but not before Bradfield Rural District Council caused a stink, so to speak, by announcing plans to build their own sewage works. This was to be at Scours Lane, between the railway and the River Thames. This was just upwind of the area now known as the Thameside Promenade, which Reading had just bought as a recreational area for its population. The incorporation of Tilehurst into Reading removed the need for a separate sewage works – and for wearing gasmasks while strolling beside the river.

The deal that was finally struck gave Caversham residents rates that were 7d lower than Reading's for the first fifteen years after incorporation, and promised a new 45 foot wide bridge across the Thames within five years and a new footbridge to Lower Caversham. Bridge Street and Church Street were both to be widened and part of the kink taken out of Berry's Corner. However, events on the continent in 1914 were to interfere with some of these promises.

Thameside Promenade in about 1920. The Council bought it for the recreation of its citizens in 1907.

The order for incorporation came into effect on 9 November 1911. A few days before, Caversham Urban District Council met for the last time. One of their final acts was to approve the abortive expenditure that had gone on opposing the incorporation. A presentation was made by a group of ratepayers to Mr Dryland, the Council Chairman, to mark his efforts in resisting the overtures of Reading. Their last business done, the entire Council retired to the Caversham Bridge Hotel for a smoking concert. Reading Borough Council, for its part, was busy choosing the first mayor for the new town of more than 90,000 people – an area they chose to refer to as Greater Reading.

MORE MOTORING MADNESS

But not everybody's minds were on local government boundaries. That bunch of hooligans, the motorists, had discovered a new way of terrorising innocent cyclists and equestrians:

Motors v Balloon: an exciting chase

The conquest of the air has resulted in a considerable addition to the possibilities for sport; for it was essentially a sporting event that had its early stages in Reading on Saturday afternoon, when seven motor cars started on an exciting balloon chase. The contest was arranged by the Berkshire Aeronautical Club and was the subject of considerable interest. The balloon was filled at the Reading Gasworks, and the occupant of the car was that well-known aeronaut, the Honourable C.S. Rolls.

As 'the hare', Mr Rolls gave the seven motor cars which followed him a good run. . . . the balloon and its solitary occupant rose from the ground amid the applause from the knot of spectators. . . . the motors were soon in full flight – as far as the restrictions of traffic allowed. There was a south-east wind blowing when the chase commenced, and the balloon was consequently carried away in the direction of Oxford, and in a few minutes was lost to view. The conditions of the chase were that the balloon should descend about 25 miles from the starting point or, if a light wind blew, at the hour of 4.30.

The Honourable C.S. Rolls had in his possession three cards, which he handed to the first three motorists who reached him after his descent, and these cards entitled the holders to the three prizes offered by the Club. . . . It finally descended at Cumnor, a few miles out of Oxford. Within a very few minutes of its coming down two motor cars had reached it, and had thus demonstrated the practicability of a balloon being chased by motor cars – at any rate, providing the wind is not too strong.

GAS LIGHTS AND TOXIC TOTS

The benefits of gas (for lighting, as opposed to aeronautical purposes) were not universally appreciated at this time. The Reading Electrical Supply Company, no doubt in a selfless piece of public information, produced a series of advertisements warning of the hideous poisons that gas lighting pumped into the atmosphere. According to them, this 'baneful product' both 'poisoned the air' and led to lung diseases, through the release of carbonic acids and sulphretted hydrogen. They warned parents not to use it in their children's bedrooms. The local gas company was stung into producing rival advertisements, claiming not only that their product was as safe as electricity, but also that it was a lot cheaper.

VOTES FOR WOMEN

Not all was sweetness and light, either, in the auction rooms on Friar Street. A suffragette, a Miss Lelacheur of Checkendon, had refused to pay

The Reading Electrical Supply Company produced a series of advertisements warning of the hideous poisons that gas lighting pumped into the atmosphere

This shop in West Street, photographed in about 1911, was the Reading headquarters of the suffragettes.

her taxes until she was given the vote. In consequence, she suffered the painful experience of having her chattels distrained. Goods to the value of £8 11s (a table, a desk and a farm cart) had been seized and were to be auctioned to secure the back taxes. Suffragettes picketed the building and some infiltrated the auction itself, with the evident intention of disrupting it. The auctioneers defused the situation by allowing one of the suffragettes' leaders to make a short speech to those present before the auction – this appeared to have no discernible effect on the bidding, which made more than the target sum. The protesters met in the Palmer Hall afterwards where, it can safely be assumed, agreement was reached that the Government should give votes to women.

CORONATION CAPERS
In June 1911 the coronation of George V and Queen Mary took place and Reading people joined the celebrations enthusiastically. A so-called State Procession of friendly societies made its way to St Mary's Church on the previous Sunday. It took place in a pitiless and relentless downpour which robbed it of much of its spectacular interest and numerical strength and greatly depleted the numbers of spectators. Those who braved the elements were rewarded by a grand parade led by the local police and the band of the Royal Berkshire Regiment. Behind them marched the Caversham Veterans' Association, a fine assortment of Aldermen and Councillors, and a bevy of friendly societies, including the Order of Buffaloes, the Oddfellows, the Order of Rechabites, a bunch of Druids and the Temperance Band. For the most part, they did not wear their finery, since the rain would have played havoc with their regalia. If all of this were not spectacular enough, the assembled masses could also enjoy the Medical Officer of Health, the Tramways Engineer and the Inspector of Weights and Measures, no doubt parading in whatever exotic outfits went with their jobs.

Later, the Caversham Veterans' Association joined another procession – this one offering a meal at the end of it. In Caversham Road they linked up with the aged poor of Reading to process to the Town Hall. There (or in the Tram Hall for the overflow party) some 1,500 of the deserving poor of the town sat down to a meal that was not so much square as positively cubic. While the Town Hall organ (or an orchestra, depending on which party you were in) serenaded them, they tucked into a menu of roast beef, boiled beef, roast lamb, veal and ham, meat pies (it was a bad day to be vegetarian), pickles and salads, hot plum puddings, pastry, stewed fruit and custard, cheese and biscuits, beer and ginger beer. A host of stewards, including worthies such as aldermen and local vicars, waited on them. Four thousand children at the town's infant schools were treated to high tea, followed in some cases by games in the local park. Only Redlands School, closed due to diphtheria, missed out on the fun. All the scholars received coronation mugs as souvenirs.

In Tilehurst, the Coronation Festivities Committee staged a celebration sports day. The list of events for adults suggests that the maintenance of dignity was not at the top of their agenda. They included the 100 yards for ladies over forty; musical chairs; the 80-yard sack race; a consolation race (imagine coming last in that); something called a bun and bottle race; a lady and poodle race (won by N.H. Saul and Miss Stevens, either of which sounds an odd name for a poodle) and a decorated bicycle competition.

Even the inmates of the Workhouse were not forgotten. The over-sixties among them were given permission to go out into the town and watch the festivities, and they were all entertained by the Spring Gardens Band and given a coronation supper, which concluded with the men being given tobacco and the women sweets and fruit. The Chairman of the Board of Guardians made a speech in which he told the residents about a former inmate of the workhouse who had recently obtained a degree from London University. A 93-year-old inmate attracted great attention by virtue of the fact that he was celebrating his fifth coronation. He had been born during the later years of King George III, during the Regency.

LEARNING FINDS A NEW SEAT

Reading's University College had its origins in art classes run in West Street as long ago as 1860. By 1911 it had become a flourishing educational establishment, based on a site at London Road. In July of that year, an endowment fund of £200,000 was given to it, partly by Lady Wantage but mostly by the Palmer family. The money was to be used to develop work of a university standard in the arts, sciences and agriculture. In particular its work was to be of benefit to the town of Reading and the surrounding counties. Within four years, it was anticipated, the College would be in a position to seek a charter as a proper university (another plan that was blown off course by the First World War).

Workers in the Huntley & Palmer factory received the news of this endowment with anger. The factory had gone through a difficult time in the past year – employees in the manufacturing department had scarcely had six full weeks' work in the past twelve months – and many were finding it hard to feed and clothe their families. They felt that, if the Palmer family really wanted to use their money to benefit the town, there were far more direct ways of doing it.

A 93-year-old inmate attracted great attention by virtue of the fact that he was celebrating his fifth coronation

WAR

War is declared, inconsiderately adding to the difficulties of the River Thames boating trade. German spies are hunted down throughout Reading and local shopkeepers do their bit for the war effort – by putting prices up.

Think of a single image to encapsulate that last golden summer of 1914, before the clouds of war darkened the skies over Europe. It might well be of a young man, oblivious to the horrors of the trenches that lay before him, punting his girl down the Thames on a sunny afternoon. Not so, according to this hire boat proprietor in July 1914:

The Charm of the River. Is it on the Wane?
. . . . a Taplow boat proprietor . . . interviewed by a press representative, gave it as his opinion that the popularity of the Thames was on the wane. The principal reason to which this doleful gentleman ascribes this state of affairs is that 'all the young sparks are on the road now. They've got their cars or motor-bicycles, and they seem to like blazing along the road better than taking it easily in a punt' is his contention and it is not improbable that, at some of our riverside resorts, there may be something to be said for this view.
  'Things are so bad . . . that I can't bear to walk up to the road and see all the motors going past. Why, there are even girls who'll hang on the back of a motorbike instead of making themselves comfortable in one of my punts.'

Hitherto, complaints about the spread of car ownership had tended to be the exclusive preserve of London cabbies and country saddlers. But the cinemas also had something to answer for, according to our complainant: 'If the weather is dull, people say "We won't go to the river, we will go to the pictures", whereas a few years ago they would have chanced getting a bit wet.'
  One of his fellow hirers recalled fondly a time when life in Reading was a barren wasteland of boredom: 'I can remember the time when there was

Berkshire Yeomanry in August 1914, pictured in Great Knollys Street.

Soldiers in Friar Street early in the First World War.

nothing to do in Reading but go on the river, but now if the weather is unsettled they turn into a picture house.'

There were more private launches on the Thames, but our laughing boys could see no good in them, either: 'They're owned by rich people who've got a bit tired of their motor cars . . .'. According to these prophets of riparian doom, the private owners spent all their time speeding up and down the Thames, creating a hazard for other river users; all of this without creating any real income for honest tradesmen such as themselves. It must have been nice for them to have something new to complain about. Up until then, all they could really moan about was the weather.

In the Forbury Gardens, members of the Royal Berkshire Regiment and survivors of the Afghan Wars of 1879/80 were laying wreaths at the foot of the lion monument, which commemorates the sacrifice made by 328 members of the regiment at the battle of Maiwand. But everybody was thinking about the war which seemed more inevitable by the day. In the stop press of the 5 August edition of the *Chronicle* there appeared the ominous news: 'It is officially announced that Great Britain has required Germany to give satisfactory reply – by midnight tonight – that she will not violate Belgian neutrality.' By the time the paper was on sale on the streets German troops had already crossed the frontier and Britain was at war.

PRICES IN READING

They say that the first casualty of war is truth. The second is grocery prices: 'As a result of the war cables, prices of provisions are rising in all parts of the country. The price of a quartern loaf will, it is announced, go up a halfpenny in London next Tuesday, and it is not to be supposed that the provinces will escape an equal, if not greater, increase. Enquiries made last night from a well-known Reading provision merchant yielded the information that at present the war had made very little difference to local retail prices.

'But,' added our informant, 'it is bound to do so within a very short time. You cannot buy any sugar at the present time,' he said, 'or even get an offer. One of the biggest men in the London trade did not open up his premises at all today and another, after putting up his prices, shut up after ten minutes. Sugar will be affected as much or more than anything. Flour is anything from 2s to 5s dearer, wheat went up again today and the prices of bacon, butter and foreign eggs are all affected. The increase in the price of bacon was stated to be nearly 1s 2d a pound.

'Some of the largest bakers in Reading have, we understand, good stocks of flour, and are determined to keep the price of bread at its present figure as long as possible.'

But none of them had stocks that would last until November 1918, and few would have believed that the war they were entering would continue that long. Popular sentiment had it that it would be over by Christmas and that, meanwhile, it was 'business as usual'.

Perhaps not quite as usual. Reading MP Captain Leslie Wilson did not give the kind of speech one normally expects at the opening of a Conservative and Unionist Party garden fête at Earley Court:

We are undoubtedly face to face with the greatest national crisis this country has ever known. . . . This country should offer a united front in the face of common danger and I recognise, as everyone in Reading would recognise, that the Government is not the Government of a party, but at the present time is the Government of the nation. I believe I echo the sentiments of every man and woman throughout the length and breadth of the country when I say that we have never sought war. I, who have known the horrors of war, have no wish to see my fellow countrymen involved in a war at any time, but if we cannot get peace with honour, then there is nothing else for it but war!

'I, who have known the horrors of war, have no wish to see my fellow countrymen involved in a war at any time, but if we cannot get peace with honour, then there is nothing else for it but war'

His words were greeted with ringing cheers, even though he forgot to declare the fête open.

War preparations were soon evident in Reading. Local men in the Navy, at home on leave, were swiftly recalled to Portsmouth or Devonport. Time-expired Royal Navy men and members of the Royal Navy Reserve were also called up and the Government announced powers to commandeer any vessel required for the war effort (no doubt giving our friend with the punts something else to complain about).

The Fourth Battalion Berkshire Regiment was recalled to Reading in the early hours of the morning from its training camp at Marlow. Members of the Territorial Army, many of them still in civilian clothes, assembled at the Drill Hall in St Mary's Butts to await their orders. Meanwhile, their commanders up at Yeomanry House on Castle Hill were still working out their plan of campaign. They were very soon on the move:

Affecting scenes, reminiscent of the South African War, were witnessed on the station platforms. As the trains steamed in, wives and sweethearts with tear-bedimmed eyes eagerly embraced their loved ones and, as the trains started, many of the women broke down. . . .

It was not until the evening that the Territorials took their departure. By seven o' clock, the first detachments began to arrive, and after being drawn up opposite the King Edward VII statue for some time, they made their way through the station gates to the accompaniment of much cheering. The crowd as a whole took

Men of the Royal Berkshire Regiment in St Mary's Butts in August 1914.

the leave-taking seriously and only when the final word of command was given for the troops to march was there anything in the nature of a public demonstration. The arrival of one sturdy-looking section just after eight o' clock and the martial notes of the bugle band helped put the crowd in better spirits, but there was more cheerfulness on the faces of the Territorials than on the majority of the countenances of those who witnessed their departure.

The mayor and mayoress were there to wish them God speed and safe return, and the passengers of trains stopping in the station leaned out of their windows and cheered the troops marshalled on the platforms. The colonel's horse was loaded into a goods wagon, along with the ammunition, trenching shovels and twenty-four boxes of Huntley & Palmer's biscuits, and the band played for the troops as they boarded. Last but not least the band themselves boarded, without any musical accompaniment. They were also going to the front, to act as stretcher-bearers.

Within the very first days of war, the newspaper switched effortlessly into propaganda mode:

Tommy Atkins has been the man of the moment in Reading this week and the breast of many a youthful territorial must have swelled with pride at the cheers which the uniform he wears have

Men of the Berkshire Yeomanry prepare for a kit inspection in Friar Street in August 1914.

occasioned. In the past, the passing of a company of our citizen soldiers would have aroused little interest and no enthusiasm. The references of the unthoughtful may sometimes have been far from complimentary, but when Britain's last efforts to secure peace failed and war was officially declared between this country and Germany, the Territorials, as a force for home defence, assumed a new importance and many a young civilian has been heard to express a regret that he has never joined their ranks.

Shades of Kipling's 'But it's "thank you, Mr Atkins", when the band begins to play'. There was propaganda, too, as the Reservists reported for duty:

. . . alert, well-built men, they commanded the admiration of those who assembled outside the barrack gates to witness their arrival. Here was a burly navvy; here, a weather-beaten son of the soil, straight from the harvest field; and there, the no less healthy and alert artisan. . . . some of them brought what was required wrapped in handkerchiefs. What struck the observer was the note of quiet determination on the faces of the men as they jauntily swung into the barracks. Some of the lively spirits rolled up singing such popular airs as 'Fall in and Follow Me' and 'I don't care what becomes of me'.

Who needed guns? We could clearly beat the Hun with sheer charisma! But there was also the need for those who stayed behind to live up to the example set by our fighting men, and the editorial column had some advice on that score:

The Call to Britons. England expects every man to do his duty
We are confident that every soldier and sailor in His Majesty's service will bear himself bravely in the hour of trial. But what about those at home? They can all help and must do their utmost to assist their country through the long period of stress that is inevitably before us. This can be done in many ways. First of all, let their patriotism and enthusiasm be tempered by sobriety of conduct. Mafficking* is not only unseemly but foolish. There is a time of great adversity and struggle before this country, and it should be met orderly, quietly and manfully. Foolish demonstrations and excitement should be religiously avoided. Panic of every form must be eschewed. . . . Any rush to draw money from the banks is strongly to be deprecated. There can be no more fatal policy than to hoard gold. . . . Then again, those who are endeavouring at all costs to lay up huge stocks of food are acting selfishly. It is only causing a huge rise in prices and a depletion of stocks. . . . Every effort should be made to keep things going normally as far as possible.

*Mafficking: a term used to describe the excessively triumphant behaviour of the London crowds on the news of the relief of Mafeking, on 17 May 1900, during the Boer War.

That last piece of advice in particular fell on deaf ears. The people of Reading went on an orgy of panic-buying that pushed prices up to near-famine levels.

The butchers had an interesting rationale for their pricing policy. According to them, it had become necessary to put the price of meat up 'in order to ensure, as far as possible, a regular supply' and 'to safeguard the interests of the consumer'. How nice of them to think of our interests! Apparently, due to problems with getting meat delivered into the town, only a third of local demand could be met. That delivery problem may have been due in part to the requisitioning of many of the horses which in those days helped turn the wheels of commerce. For example, in the same week that Simonds' Brewery lost thirty-five of its staff to the army, thirty-two of their horses were also called up for military duty. The problems were compounded by people posing as Government officials and falsely requisitioning people's horses. Farmers were advised that only police constables would do the requisitioning, and would do so armed with a magistrate's warrant. All others should be ignored.

But one possible solution to the food shortage was at hand. Suttons announced that they were carrying out trials of radioactive materials to test their potential for making plants grow more strongly. They had bought several hundredweight of radioactive ore and were using it to grow flowers and vegetables on their London Road trial grounds. They were holding an exhibition of their results for the local dignitaries, preceded by a lunch. (Presumably the guests were able to read the menu by the light from the lettuce.)

1914 – Kitchener was not yet pointing his finger from the posters.

Your King and Country Need You.

Will you answer your Country's Call? Each day is fraught with the gravest possibilities, and at this very moment the Empire is on the brink of the greatest war in the history of the world.

In this crisis your Country calls on all her young unmarried men to rally round the Flag and enlist in the ranks of her Army.

If every patriotic young man answers her call, England and her Empire will emerge stronger and more united than ever.

If you are unmarried and between 18 and 30 years old will you answer your Country's Call? and go to the nearest Recruiter— whose address you can get at any Post Office, and

Join the Army To-day!

Recruitment for the armed forces began to affect the town in all sorts of ways. Reading Football Club lost a centre-half (Dickenson) and a full-back (Millership) in a single week. In the same period, Huntley & Palmer lost two hundred employees to the forces. The recruitment offices were breaking all the records set during the South African War: during a single ninety-minute spell that same week, fifty-five Reading men were signed up.

One bizarre aspect of the patriotic fervour of the times was the tendency for deserters to report back for duty. In one example, George Barry, who had deserted from his regiment in 1897, almost twenty years before, surrendered himself to the police station in Reading in order that he could have a crack at the new enemy. Given that he had deserted before the Boer War even started, he can hardly have claimed that the army had denied him an opportunity to shoot at foreigners.

Employers made arrangements to look after those of their staff who were doing their patriotic duty in the armed forces. Huntley & Palmer set up weekly visits to the families of serving staff to ensure there was no hardship. Having said that, there was no doubt a good deal of hardship among those staff who remained at work in the factory. The loss of export orders due to the war forced them to put male staff on three-quarter time and female staff on half time (the latter meant a 24 hour week, slightly less than half the then-standard 54 hour working week). Part of the factory's production was switched to making army ration biscuits and another to the manufacture of shells for the guns.

Suttons gave an undertaking to look after the wives and children of their serving employees and to keep their positions open until their return. They also launched an appeal fund, offering to match any contributions made by their employees, supporting any workers in the town put out of work or on short time as a result of the war.

Simonds' Brewery set up their own Irregular Corps among their office workers, training them in square bashing and rifle drill in case they were ever called upon to repel invaders in the factory yard. The Council's Education Committee decided to boost the salaries of those teachers who signed up, making up their wages to what they would have earned if they had stayed in the classroom. Unions lobbied the Council to set up a hardship fund to help care for the children of everyone who had been called up, or who had been put on short time as a result of the war.

The harsh reality of war manifested itself in the letters page. A letter from a reader suggested that those who lost their loved ones in the war, instead of spending a lot of money on the formal mourning clothes that were favoured at that time, should instead simply wear a black armband with a Union Jack on it. This would enable them to save their money for the difficult task of living without a breadwinner in the family.

LOOK OUT, THERE'S A HUN ABOUT!

The town suddenly became obsessed with the idea that they were surrounded by German spies: 'Owing to the fact that so many German spies are now in this country, the strictest watch is being kept at all the military depots in and around Reading. Strangers are being closely inspected, and are not being permitted to enter the grounds of the regimental depots or buildings without holding an official pass.' German residents, some of whom had been in the country for many years, were required to register under the Aliens Restriction Order 1914. Many of them applied to become naturalised Britons on the spot; many more probably also wished to do so, but the authorities may not have known about it, since some of the would-be applicants spoke no English.

Rumours of arrests of spies swept the town, and the police were sent to check out a host of suspicious aliens, most of which turned out to be complete wild goose-chases. One dubious-looking character seen measuring a wall by the railway station, no doubt calculating the size of bomb required to reduce it to rubble, turned out to be a workman erecting an advertising hoarding. A real German, employed by a Reading firm, was detained when he was found to possess several military documents, one of which was regarded as being of considerable importance. It turned out that the man was a deserter from the German army.

Technology made the menace of spies seem even greater. In 1901 Marconi had transmitted a wireless signal across the Atlantic. Although the first proper broadcasts of the British Broadcasting Corporation were still over a decade away, the potential of radio as a means of communication had not escaped the authorities. Edward Tunbridge had constructed a home-made wireless apparatus at the rear of his premises in Castle Street. With it, he was able to send and receive messages from other operators, including many from ships and from the Eiffel Tower, which had been wired up as a centre of communications for the French. Most of

One dubious-looking character seen measuring a wall by the railway station, no doubt calculating the size of bomb required to reduce it to rubble, turned out to be a workman erecting an advertising hoarding

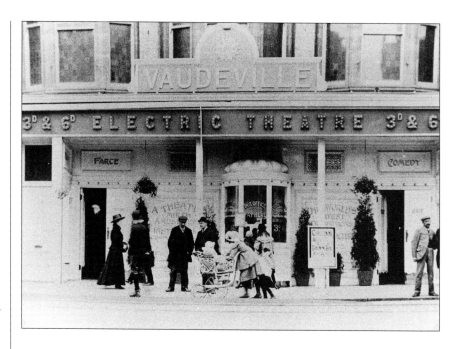

The Vaudeville Electric Theatre opened in 1909 on the north side of Broad Street, opposite Chain Street.

the messages from the Eiffel Tower were in some kind of code (possibly French?), which meant that it cannot exactly have rivalled the Archers in listener interest. But Mr Tunbridge's no doubt innocent hobby came to an abrupt halt:

On Monday, a large motor car drove up to his premises, and he was informed by a Post Office official that his wireless apparatus would have to be disconnected. The official explained that, as it would be a long business to lower the aerials and as he had many other places to visit, all that would be done would be to connect the aerials straight to earth. The various instruments used in the apparatus were stowed away in a cupboard, and upon the door was placed the official seal.

THE LURE OF THE SILVER SCREEN

The new-fangled cinemas continued to do good trade amid all the disruption of war. Among the most successful was the Vaudeville on Broad Street, which had opened in 1909. In those days they changed their programme twice a week. Among the attractions showing in August 1914 were:

The Crime in the Tunnel, a dramatic story of a murder in a tunnel, and after a useless attempt to place the crime on the shoulders of an innocent person, the bringing to justice of the culprit . . . *The Fighting Blood of 1809* – It is the story of the rising of the Tyrolese, headed by their brave leader Andreas Hofer, against the oppression of Napoleon, and the subsequent defeat and death of Andreas. Another interesting film featuring in the programme will be *Rip, the Dog Detective*. Also showing was *Tessebel of the Storm Country* starring Mary Pickford, and *Saints and their Sorrows*, a story of human passion and frailty and the noble heroism of a village parson.

Even in those days there was an appreciation that presentation sometimes mattered more than substance. In one of the odder demonstrations of anti-German feeling, the grocers Venners of Southampton Street announced that what had hitherto been known to their customers as the German sausage would now be known as the Empire sausage. And over at the local Board of Guardians, there was a debate going on about what they should call the institution they managed. In many parts of the country, it was pointed out, they had dropped the name workhouse, with its unpleasant overtones. The Chairman got very tetchy with the reformers. He demanded: "What do you want it called – Sunny Side?' The workhouse it remained, at least for the time being.

THE SOMME

1916

In the war the terrible loss of life is reaching its height and Reading men are at the centre of the conflict. Locally, some think that chanting rhymes against the Kaiser will help win the war. There is even violence from the ladies on the picket line at Huntley & Palmers.

By 1916 the Allies were in the middle of a war of attrition that was imposing staggering costs in human lives in return for negligible gains of territory. June 1916 saw the end of the battle of Verdun, in which nearly 600,000 casualties were suffered over a fortress that had no strategic significance. Similarly, the Somme made little sense as a battlefield. It was chosen as a point of attack to bolster the uneasy international alliance that held the Allies together – here, the British would form the lion's share of the attacking force (whereas the French had borne the brunt of the attack at Verdun). The attack on the Somme offered little hope of success against an enemy who held the high ground and had it heavily fortified.

The troops who would mount the attack were enthusiastic, but ill-trained – they were Lord Kitchener's volunteers, and had not been taught to shoot straight or to act independently, once scattered from their main

Reading Tramway recruits conductresses as the men go off to the war.

Officers of the 7th Battalion, Royal Berkshire Regiment. Shire Hall, February 1915.

1914 – Volunteering for a Commission greatly reduced one's chances of surviving the war.

COMMISSIONS IN THE REGULAR ARMY, SPECIAL RESERVE & TERRITORIAL FORCE.

Gentlemen resident in Reading and neighbourhood desirous of obtaining Commissions are invited to apply, either personally or by letter, to

The Officer Commanding,

Officers Training Corps,

University College, Reading.

force or deprived of command. Their immediate officers were equally raw recruits, trained largely in a code of heroism which meant that officer casualties were six times greater than those of the men they led. Every aspect of the offensive seemed designed to result in a huge and pointless waste of lives.

None the less this was what was referred to in the *Chronicle* as 'The Great Push'. By now the easy jingoism of the early years of the war had been swept away, and many pages of the paper each week were given over to pictures and stories about those Reading men who had been injured or killed for their country. Frank details of each man's injuries were published; they ranged from 'a sniper's bullet grazed his head but he soon got over it' or 'a bullet pierced his ankle and took a large piece of flesh off the heel', to 'died of shrapnel wounds'.

The Berkshire Regiment was in the thick of the battle. Letters from the front gave a vivid, and remarkably uncensored, account of the hell in which the men were fighting. Lance Corporal Allum of Foxhill Road gave his account of being wounded:

We approached a party of Germans in some shell craters and I found myself with a small party holding them at bay, with rifles, two machine-guns and bombs. A German bomb was thrown near me and a piece caught me in the mouth. That's why I am here [in hospital]; but I shall never in all my life forget the awful sights I saw that morning – dead and wounded, dying and mutilated, hands, feet, brains all in an awful confusion. Only God's merciful care saved my life; I marvel that my head wasn't blown off by that bomb; it knocked me flying.

I had to retrace my steps to the fire trench to get to the dressing station; I helped a chap back who had been hit in the leg near me. We had to get through wire, over dead men, dodge snipers and all sorts. I left him at the trench dressing station and went on to get out of the trenches; even that was a shell-dodging game. There were some ghastly sights in that trench. I can only wonder and thank God that I am alive.

In some cases they published letters from the men's commanding officers. Second Lieutenant A.F.J. Burnham had been a member of Reading Football Club and an enthusiastic player for the local YMCA Football Club. His parents received the following letter from his Captain at the beginning of July:

You will have heard by now of the gallant death of your son on the night of 28-29th, but I must write you just a line to let you know how much we all felt his death. Ever since he joined me in B Company he has been loved by officers and men alike; he was always so cheerful and full of life that he was just the man we want out here. His Platoon – number 5 – I know miss him very much, as he was always thinking of them, and it was while cheering them in the midst of a heavy bombardment that he met his death. He was just lighting a cigarette on the fire step when a shell hit the top of the parapet and then took the top of his head off; he was, of course, killed at once. He was buried yesterday in a military cemetery near here and I have just visited his grave. . . . He was such a good friend to me that I find it impossible to express my feelings at his loss, but I trust you will realise how much you are sympathised with by us all out here.

Second Lieutenant Burnham was twenty-five when he died. Only two years older than him was Private A.B. Chandler, a plasterer from Great Knollys Street, with a wife and child. He was killed just three weeks after reaching the front. Some families suffered the pain of bereavement unnecessarily – Private Percy Harrison was reported killed, but was later discovered to be in good health, a prisoner of the Germans. Rumour also spread that Sergeant J.W. Lambourn of Leopold Road had been killed.

1916 – and women are called up to the grocery front line.

'He is not even thinking of getting wounded, as he knows I cannot spare him yet awhile'

This time, his commanding officer was able to write back with better news: 'Your brother, Sergeant Lambourn of my company, is very much alive and doing exceedingly good work. He is not even thinking of getting wounded, as he knows I cannot spare him yet awhile.' One of the more ironic deaths of the campaign was that of Staff Sergeant J.H. Bennett, who did not fall victim to shell or bullet, but died at the front when an operation for appendicitis went wrong.

STICKS AND STONES . . .

If the jingoism were not quite so jaunty as in the first days of the conflict, there were still those who were ready to conduct the war by means of name-calling. Whoever dreamed up the following anti-German nursery rhymes, published in the *Chronicle*, should have faced a war crimes tribunal for offences against literature:

> Kaiser, Kaiser, quite contrary,
>   All your plans do go.
>   For Haig excels in men and shells
>   And all your schemes lays low.
> Old Hindenburg Hubbard went to the Russ cupboard
>   To get the Hun dachshund a bone;
>   But when he got there,
>   he found a strong bear
>   And so the Hun dog got none.
> Pat a Hun, Pat a Hun, khaki man,
>   So I will master, as fast as I can!
>   I'll give him a pat with a bayonet for tea,
>   And make him give three cheers for England and me!

One of the problems for the men on the battlefields was a shortage of shells and, back in Reading, the mayor announced the cancellation of the August Bank Holiday for that year, mainly so that munitions workers would keep supplying the troops without interruption.

DISCORD AMONG THE DIGESTIVES

This news would not have pleased the workers at Huntley & Palmer. Largely led by the women workers, they had picketed the factory during a three-hour strike for improved terms. The strike produced results, in that their so-called 'war bonuses' were consolidated into their basic pay, and thus counted in their overtime calculations. But there were complaints that the women had used violence in their picketing. A correspondent signing himself 'An ex-soldier' told the letters page: 'One old man of 62 had his hat knocked off and was half-throttled simply because he wished to do his bit in the factory to help keep the home fires burning. It was a trifle humorous to see a gang of girls singing "Keep the home fires burning" and at the same time handing out blows to those who wished to do what they were singing.'

Indignant factory workers replied the following week that it was impossible to keep the home fires burning on the 21 shillings a week plus 2 shillings war bonus that they were receiving. They were fighting for the Tommies, they said, to ensure that they had a civilised standard of living when they came home. Their strike was closely followed by industrial action at the town's other biscuit company, Serpells.

(Opposite) 1916 – our boys fight clean on the Western Front.

SUNLIGHT SOAP

CLEANLINESS, LIKE MUSIC, HATH CHARMS!

WHILST Tommy has no "Hymn of Hate," he hates to be dirty and loves to be clean. Sunlight Soap is a boon to clean fighters.

The clean, chivalrous fighting instincts of our gallant soldiers reflect the ideals of our business life. The same characteristics which stamp the British Tommy as the cleanest fighter in the world have won equal repute for British goods.

Sunlight Soap is typically British. It is acknowledged by experts to represent the highest standard of Soap Quality and Efficiency. Tommy welcomes it in the trenches just as you welcome it at home.

£1,000 GUARANTEE OF PURITY ON EVERY BAR.

Include a Tablet in your next parcel to the Front.

The name Lever on Soap is a Guarantee of Purity and Excellence.

LEVER BROTHERS LIMITED, PORT SUNLIGHT.

S 286—34

The Reading Tribunal was meeting regularly to hear applications for exemption from military service, usually on the grounds that the applicants were doing essential war work. C.H. Lovegrove, for example, was a member of a family of undertakers, who had contracts with the Government, among others, to bury war casualties. In another case, the job of School Attendance Officer was deemed to be work of national importance. Some exemptions had strings attached to them. People were in some cases only exempted from military service if they combined their day job with volunteer work in a hospital or as a special Police Constable.

Rationing did not affect people as it much as it did in the Second World War, and the *Chronicle*'s motoring correspondent was able to complain about the exorbitant petrol prices that were being charged, using the war as an excuse:

And I do not see much hope of a reduction after the war. That isn't the way with monopolists. They find the public will pay nearly 3s a gallon and they will continue to mulct the public as long as they can.

The cinemas continued to provide a favourite source of entertainment for many. Among the major attractions at the time of the Somme campaign was Mary Pickford, in an adaptation of Puccini's famous opera, *Madame Butterfly*. One can't help feeling that it might have lost something in the adaptation into a silent movie.

PEACE AMID THE MADNESS

Reading men in the trenches, receiving newspapers from home, must have found it painful indeed to read a lyrical account of a steamer trip along the Thames from Reading to Henley, one breathlessly hot summer's day:

'The surrounding woodlands fill the soul with quiet and peaceful joy'

The rushes and reeds by the side of the stream surmounted by the tall-growing grasses, the white umbrels of the alder bushes, the glasslike river and the surrounding woodlands fill the soul with quiet and peaceful joy, while the beautiful roses and geraniums in the lock-keeper's garden are beautiful to contemplate. . . . Soon we are passing under one of the Norman arches of the old-fashioned Sonning bridge, beloved of artists, where the church of one of the prettiest villages on the Thames nestles among the trees, almost kissed by a copper beech. . . . Just under the bridge on the right, we see the celebrated White Hart Inn standing behind 'the rose garden of the stream'. . . .

Forward the river winds among the water meadows and a cooling breeze comes from the Oxfordshire hills on our left. Now stand up and scent the new-mown hay. Yet there are fields of flowering grasses going to seed while waiting for the lady haymakers to take the place of the boys doing the fighting.

The piece went on to evoke the ancient stones of Shiplake Church, hidden among the trees; the cattle coming down to drink at the riverside; and the birds flitting among the brightly coloured wild flowers along the banks. But for many Reading men that summer, there was only the sound of guns, and the smell of mud and death.

ARMISTICE

Reading and the nation celebrate their victory with triumphalism. The town suffers its share of the worldwide influenza epidemic; women get the vote and Reading starts to provide homes fit for its heroes.

After four long years, the First World War was coming to a conclusion. The Germans had sought an Armistice in October and the following weeks were spent arguing about the terms of any peace settlement. After such a costly and bitter struggle, it was not surprising that British public opinion sought to punish the Germans for their belligerence. This editorial from the *Chronicle*, published just a few days before peace was declared and while the Germans were still arguing over the settlement, reflected the views of many at the time:

The Whining Hun

It was foretold that when the Huns had lost the war by force of arms they would endeavour to cheat their enemies of victory with tears in their eyes. . . . Did the Germans think of this when they subjected the Russians to slavery and worse at Brest-Littovsk? Did they think of it when they forced upon Romania the infamous Treaty of Bucharest? . . . Of course not. Their creed was the spoils to the victors. And it is also their creed when they have lost to endeavour to avoid the consequences by the exercise of wiles and stratagems. . . . By appealing to our sentiments and our good nature they hope to turn aside our just wrath, and from our purpose to exorcise the world from militarism. . . .

But we need have no fear. In spite of all, we do not think the Hun is going to escape. . . . all the peace talk in the world has been and is futile. We must go on

The survivors of the 2nd Battalion, Royal Berkshire Regiment, return to receive the Lord Lieutenant's congratulations, 17 May 1919.

FLU

has been conspicuous by its absence in homes where

FIRST AID

is regularly used.

FIRST AID is the scientific disinfectant soap of guaranteed power. It is made in a unique way, and its value in combating microbe-borne disease can hardly be over-estimated.

In triple tablets, 7½d.

Made only by Christr. Thomas & Bros. Ltd., Bristol

✱ **The First Aid Book, 40 pp. of illustrated first aid hints, free on request if usual dealer's name mentioned.**

1918 – Patent remedies stood little chance against the influenza epidemic.

until Germany surrenders, and then it will be in our own hands to resettle the world. We do not want to be harsh, but we should be very foolish indeed to listen to the whining Hun and let him off his punishment and reparation.

It was in sentiments like these that the seeds of the Second World War were sown. The Treaty of Versailles helped to create the economic and political conditions in which Hitler came to power. But the mood of the people of Reading was first and foremost one of celebration. At 11 a.m. on 11 November the big party began: 'Reading, in common with the rest of the country, has spent a week of rejoicing consequent upon the signing of the Armistice on Monday.'

The first intimation in Reading that the Armistice had been signed was conveyed by the blowing of long blasts on the Great Western Railway's hooter at 11 o' clock, followed in quick response by the other hooters in the neighbourhood. There was no mistaking the meaning of the welcome sound and soon people were pouring out of the offices and shops on their way to the Market Place, to await the official announcement at the *Reading Mercury*. The hoisting of Messrs Suttons' flag was the sign of the confirmation of the good tidings and the delight displayed by all the inhabitants showed how great was the relief that the four years of terrible strain was over. . . .

The Mayor's official announcement of the official signing of the Armistice was received with great cheering and the waving of flags. The Deputy Mayor said they had passed through a time which he hoped they would never pass through again. They had now the peace which they had been longing for. Now let them see in connection with peace what they could do to solve the great problems before them. Let them set to work and make the England they all admired the place they so greatly desired it to be (Great cheering). 'Rule Britannia' was lustily sung and the proceedings terminated.

The marvellous thing was the rapidity with which the flags made their appearance, alike on the business premises and private dwellings, and in the possession of the drivers of vehicles and pedestrians. . . . A string of flags made their appearance across Broad Street and . . . tradesmen's carts were profusely and effectively decorated. All sorts of discordant musical instruments were soon brought into requisition, and the streets resounded to the din of whistles and trumpets and rattles and indeed of 'any old thing' which could add to the general expression. Impromptu processions were speedily organised and in these exhilarating touring parties soldiers, wounded and otherwise, appeared to take a conspicuous share. . . . Officers were quite as eager to show their delight as the men and there were some novel impromptu methods displayed of showing pleasure. One officer was wearing a Uhlan's helmet, and other trophies from the front were brought out to show satisfaction that the Bosch was finally discomfited. . . . The female population were particularly demonstrative, and it was apparent that in many cases they had left work almost en masse. The general outburst of rejoicing at the good news put out of the question all desire for work in a great many factories and business houses, and many firms and shops closed early in the day.

The Chief Constable received the official instruction that the masking of street lamps might be removed and that the total number of lamps in use could be increased to one-half. It was also arranged that the whole of the lamps in the centre of the town should be lit. The effect was at once apparent, especially as the shading of lights in shops and houses had been withdrawn. . . .

It is many years since Broad Street witnessed such scenes as were enacted there on Monday evening. For several hours, it was the venue for an impromptu but none the less effective firework display. . . . It was amazing where all the squibs and rockets came from. . . . As soon as the streets were sufficiently dark, the fun began. Some hundreds of fireworks must have been discharged in all varieties. There were detonators which threatened hardened warriors with shell-shock when they exploded in close proximity to their heels, rockets which sailed gracefully into the sky, thunderflashes which created quite a furore, squibs, crackers and coloured lights all added to the general display, while the side door of the Oatsheaf

1918 – Heelas offer custom-made memorials for war heroes.

and other places of vantage were utilised for the discharge of Catherine wheels. . . .

The utmost good humour prevailed, and it speaks well for the whole of the population that there was not the slightest attempt at disorder. . . . There was certainly a great comparison in the harmlessness of the exuberance on Monday evening with the wildness of the Mafeking manifestations. . . .

A remarkable scene was witnessed in Flint Street, where a gang of German prisoners were engaged in brick loading and hauling. When the news came to them, they cheered as frantically as the guard did who had charge of them.

One lady in a business house in Oxford Street, having neither dog nor cat to decorate, gaily bedecked a tame rabbit with streamers of the national colours, which she proudly exhibited to her customers.

We saw but one effigy of the Kaiser, on which was the wording 'The German madman run amok'. There was hooting for it wherever it was seen. It was burnt in St Mary's Butts.

But not everybody could join in the celebrations. Mrs E.L. Davies was burying her husband even as the bells were ringing for the victory celebrations. Evan Lloyd Davies, a schoolteacher at the Wokingham Road Senior School, had volunteered for the Royal Berkshire Regiment at the outbreak of war. He was seriously wounded by shrapnel, but recovered and returned to duty. At the Battle of the Somme, his gallantry earned him the Military Medal. It also cost him a serious head injury, which left him convalescing at a nursing home in Newbury for a full two years. But he still required an operation to his head, and it was this that finally took his life.

Others were suffering from something no less deadly than the war:

The Influenza: Ravages in Reading
The influenza was at its worst in Reading and district on Tuesday this week . . . although it was reported to be on the wane elsewhere, it was still bad in Reading.

Decorated bicycles form part of the 1918 Armistice celebrations.

On Saturday a woman named Trussle of Finch Buildings, who had been unwell for some time, and who was attacked at the beginning of last week with the influenza, rose from her bed and fell on the outhouse below, from which she rolled into the garden and, her fall being broken, she received no serious injury. She was rendered unconscious, however, and was badly bruised. Local officers with a doctor visited her and as a means of 'self-protection' she has been admitted to the infirmary. . . .

On Monday morning, there was a queue at Dr Fosbery's surgery in the Oxford Road, which extended round the corner of Kensington Road. It must have measured at least 70 yards.

We are informed that rather over a third of the postmen and postwomen are suffering from the attack. Those who are able to carry out their duties are very much harassed, and their heavy labours are telling upon them.

The insurance companies are being very hard hit. In one office alone – a prominent office near this office – nearly £200 had been paid out in death claims (most of them for quite small amounts) before midday on Tuesday.

The different railway companies have suffered badly. The men untouched, however, have placed their shoulders to the wheel in gallant fashion, and passenger and goods traffic have not been interfered with to any perceptible degree.

Mr Farrant, a farmer from Mortimer, has lost a son and a daughter.

At its height, the influenza epidemic was causing three thousand deaths a week in London alone.

HOMES FIT FOR HEROES

At the end of any great conflict there is a tendency to look critically at the order of peacetime society. On this occasion, it meant that the troops would return home to the promise of 'homes fit for heroes'. In Reading's case, it meant in particular the announcement of plans by the Council to

Reading Corporation housing department's plan of houses for the Shinfield and Norcot Estates, c. 1918.

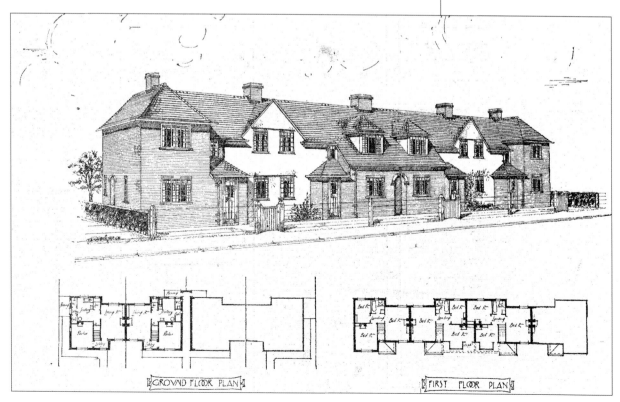

GROUND FLOOR PLAN   FIRST FLOOR PLAN

Homes unfit for heroes. These houses in Bath Court are awaiting demolition, c. 1935.

build five hundred homes for the working classes. They rejected the offer of a site by the Swan Hotel at Burghfield and opted instead for Ayres' Farm, on the east side of the Basingstoke Road, at Whitley: 'The land is pleasing in character, is well situated for drainage, is within about ten minutes' walk of the existing tram terminus and is on the bus route.'

They were offered the 50 acre site at £220 per acre, provided they completed the purchase within one year of the signing of the peace with Germany. If there were any doubts about the need for improved housing for the workers, they were answered one night in early December of 1918:

Partial Collapse of Housing: Exciting Scenes in Bosier Square
Ample evidence that better tenements are necessary in the town was afforded early on Sunday morning when three houses in Bosier Square – a thickly populated neighbourhood in Coley – partially collapsed. The wonder is that no one was killed. Suddenly, and practically without any warning, beyond a slight sound of cracking, the roofs of the houses . . . crashed in. A number of people were in their beds at the time and the scene for some minutes was one of panic. One of the women occupants, in her night attire, with her baby child in arms, rushed from her house in considerable alarm, quickly to be given kindly shelter by a neighbour. . . . In addition to the roofs falling in, portions of the outer walls gave way, and fell into the pathway below, whilst ominous-looking cracks in the building are discernible. The houses have been shored up and everything possible to prevent further mishap has been done. During the whole of Sunday, crowds of people visited the scene.

Huntley & Palmer were also party to the postwar new deal for working people. They announced that plans to introduce improved working conditions for their staff, put on hold because of the war, were finally to be put into effect. The basic working week was to come down from 54 to 48 hours, and staff who had been employed by them for at least three years (and war service counted for this purpose) qualified for a week's paid holiday each year. If this were not enough, they also announced new rates of pay for their staff. Men (or, rather, boys) started at 18s for a 48 hour week at the age of fourteen, rising to 45s aged eighteen. Women were not quite equal, starting at 17s at fourteen, and rising (in the manufacturing department at least) to 30s at the age of twenty-one. When the unions heard of these new terms, they received them with acclaim and proposed a vote of thanks to the company and their union officials.

Parliament had been sitting for a record length of time when the war ceased, and a general election was called immediately. One of the election's most important features was that many women would be able to vote in it for the first time. However, the *Chronicle* showed remarkably little interest in this major extension of the franchise. The main coverage given to the women's vote in early December got about half the space devoted to the candidates' positions on temperance. It appeared that the candidates 'have replied in the affirmative to a number of questions put by the Women's Local Government Society and the National Union of Women's Suffrage. The questions dealt with the removal of all disabilities of women with respect to local government, their appointment as J.P.s and on Royal Commissions and on Parliamentary and Departmental Committees; also the equality of women on questions of social morality, etc.' But the electorate seemed much more interested in which party would hang the Kaiser and make Germany pay.

The electorate seemed much more interested in which party would hang the Kaiser and make Germany pay

THE GENERAL STRIKE   1926

The General Strike brings civil disorder in Reading, disrupting royal visits to the town. The Whitley Whiff is born and a Reading man captains England at cricket.

Trying to glean information about the General Strike from contemporary newspaper reports is fraught with difficulty, since the newspaper workers were among the firmest supporters of the strike. The only local paper to be published in Reading while the strike was on was the Socialist *Reading Citizen*, an irony that was not lost on the strike's opponents. The following account has been compiled from reports of the events of the strike, printed when newspaper production resumed.

Reading was fortunate in having a relatively prosperous economy at the time. Maximum unemployment in recent years had peaked in 1921, when some four thousand people had been out of work. It was not to get that high again between the wars, not even during the years of the depression in the 1930s (when the figure stood at around 2,500, or 8 per cent of the workforce). This was, perhaps, reflected in the rather patchy response locally to the strike call. The railways came out firmly for the strike, as did the tramway staff (with at least one notable exception, as we shall see), the building workers and the workers at Simonds' Brewery. But the electric

The Perfect Food-Drink

Simonds famous Milk Stout is the ideal drink for the Rheumatic, Invalids and all Workers. Every pint of this nourishing beverage contains the body building Carbo-Hydrates of 10 ounces of Pure Dairy Milk.

SIMONDS MILK STOUT

THE HOP LEAF

H. & G. SIMONDS, LTD.,
BREWERS, WINE AND SPIRIT MERCHANTS, READING. *Established over 120 years.*
Telephone No. 1430 Reading (3 lines).   Telegrams: "Simonds, Reading."

1926 – Drink enough of this, and you could live for ever!

and gas companies, the biscuit factory Serpells and the metal box manufacturers Huntley Boorne & Stevens carried on working as usual.

The town was, however, affected in various other ways by the disruption. The Prince of Wales postponed his trip to the Borough to open the long-delayed replacement Caversham Bridge, originally promised as a part of the boundary extension of 1911 – the mayor had to open it instead; the town centre was reported to be deserted on Saturday night and even the annual dinner of the Reading and District Billiards League was cancelled. The Rotary Club did meet during the strike, but felt it necessary to offer an elaborate justification for doing so. Canon Gillmor explained to the meeting how the application of the principles of Rotarianism could go a long way towards solving the present industrial problems.

Some services were staffed by 'volunteers'. (The strikers had a different name for them.) Their motivation may have been the uniform, as much as any ideological position. At the station amateur porters fought one another for the chance to wear the limited supply of railwaymen's hats, and about seven hundred Reading people volunteered to become Special Police Constables. Volunteers also drove the trams, with a police escort to protect them from irate strikers. The escort was needed, too, one day in the centre of Reading when:

. . . a large crowd became hostile to men taking tramcars into the depot, and also to the police escort. As a result six employees of the Reading Corporation Tramways who were on strike were charged at the Reading Police Court on Wednesday. . . .

About 8.45, when the cars were being brought in, a large crowd collected in Duke Street and London Street. As soon as the cars appeared, there was a very considerable booing and shouting, and half a brick was thrown at a tramcar. A minor scrimmage took place and a police sergeant and constable were assaulted. . . . The crowd was very hostile and numbered roughly between 400 and 500 people. . . . there were cries of 'Pull these blacklegs off the trams'.

Crowds in Market Place listen to trades union organiser Ben Russell during the General Strike of 1926.

One of the demonstrators, whom the police alleged had punched one of their officers in the back, claimed in court that he had simply clutched hold of the constable when he slipped in the road. Whatever the truth of the matter, three of the six were found not guilty and only one – who had tried to derail the tram by interfering with the tramlines – received a custodial sentence. He was also the only one not to be reinstated after the strike by the tramcar company. The tramway company later paid a gratuity of £2 to each of their employees who remained at work during the strike.

Some employees may have felt that their £2 was rather hard-earned. Archibald Arding of 'Emdean 'Ill (sorry, Hemdean Hill) was accused of threatening Robert Deas, who worked as a coachbuilder for the Tramways. Deas owed rent money and decided to return to work before the strike was officially called off. Arding visited Deas' home while he was at work and made threats to his wife, as a result of which Deas returned home under police protection. Arding returned to Deas' house that same evening and spoke to Robert Deas himself. After making dark allusions to some awful fate about to befall the tramways themselves, he told the strike-breaker: 'You have done a serious thing. I have had a job from keeping the men from coming round and throwing you in the river. When you get back you will have a hell of a life from the foremen and the men and your life in Reading won't be worth living, so that you can clear out

Caversham Bridge, Reading. The new ferro-concrete bridge being paved, looking towards Caversham, 1926.

as soon as you like.' He added for good measure that two or three hundred men were planning to come round and 'pull him out' and that he, Arding, would do nothing to stop them.

Arding's version of events was rather different. He claimed he told Deas that he would lose his trade union benefit and would be expelled from the Society. He did not use any intimidation, though he may have told Mrs Deas that he hoped the men would not molest her husband. He might also just have mentioned that, as her husband was out of a union, he might find it difficult to find employment in Reading. Oh yes, and it was just conceivable that he might have let slip the fact that, as the defendant was coming out of his Union under such disgraceful conditions, his life in Reading would be very uncomfortable. The jury found him guilty of intimidation and he was sentenced to one month's hard labour, complaining as he was sent down that he was being made a scapegoat for the entire Reading branch of his Union.

One 'volunteer' gave the newspaper an account of his time as a lorry driver during the strike. His efforts, in a lorry that could have been used as a prop by circus clowns, hardly seemed likely to bring down the trade union movement. During the course of his journeys he had to secure both the door and the windscreen in place with string, stop at every pond and puddle to fill the leaking radiator, and fix innumerable punctures. At one point, his load slid off the flat back of the lorry while it was labouring up a hill. He himself did not encounter any direct hostility from the public

Don't forget the Showery Days.

Our New Raincoats are all that could be desired. They are proofed, cut and made by experts. Every good thing and every new shade is here for inspection. They keep you dry on wet days, and keep out the cold on chilly days. The popular Four-in-One is here too, absolutely guaranteed to resist the weather.

We invite you to call round and make an inspection.

GARRETT'S for Raincoats
NUMBER THIRTEEN, WEST STREET, READING.

1926 – Men's fashions from one of Reading's lost retailers.

but in London strike-breakers were stoned and forced to abandon their journeys.

The strike did, however, have its humorous moments. One picket line reported a striker who came and pleaded with them to be allowed back into work, rather than having to spend any more time at home with his wife. Another man took up the offer of a lift to work. He found himself one of five occupants of a two-seater car with no discernible brakes (the driver used the gears to slow down) and no horn (the driver announced his presence by banging his fist loudly on the door of the car). He arrived at work a broken man, but one with a fuller appreciation of the joys of public transport.

During the strike the protesters were kept occupied by a May Day demonstration, which paraded from the Trade Union Club in Minster Street through the streets of Reading to King's Meadow for a rally. King's Meadow was also the venue for an inter-union football tournament for those involved in the dispute.

The strike ended with a gradual – and uneasy – return to work:

AFTER THE STRIKE: DIFFICULTIES IN READING

Although the General Strike was called off at 1.15 on Wednesday, conditions on Thursday in Reading, as in the country generally, were very little better than the previous day. The railwaymen, men in the building trade, many of the tramwaymen and several printers were still out.

Railway companies have given notice in some districts that because of the coal stoppage it will not be possible to give employment to the full staff, and some private firms have stated that they are unable to take back all their men until orders increase. It is denied, however, that there is any intention to cut wages.

The railwaymen insist on the reinstatement of full staffs, and the same attitude has been taken in other industries.

Reinstatement was by no means automatic. The railwaymen extended their strike because of conditions attached to their re-employment. Tramwaymen were only taken back on as and when required, and their employers 'reserved their rights' in relation to the fact that they had broken their contracts of employment. The Government, too, was unwilling to force reinstatement upon employers, saying that: 'H.M. Government has no power to compel employers to take back every man who has gone on strike; that displacements were unavoidable in view of the state of business in consequence of the strike, and that many employers had entered into agreements with volunteers. Attention is, however, drawn to the hope expressed by the Prime Minister in his statement in the House of Commons, that we should resume our work in a spirit of cooperation, putting behind us all malice and all vindictiveness.'

ROYALTY GALORE

In June 1926 Huntley & Palmer celebrated their centenary in grand style. In the morning the Prince of Wales made his delayed visit to the factory. His name was entered in the visitors' book, along with those of his grandfather, Edward VII (who came as Prince of Wales in 1882) and his father, King George V (1918). In the afternoon all the staff were given an extra week's wages in celebration and in the evening the management retired to the Great Western Hotel for a lavish banquet, which concluded with a toast to the King and the singing of the National Anthem. The

Visit of the Prince of Wales to Reading, 1926. The royal car is shown passing Huntley & Palmer's biscuit factory in King's Road.

senior management were fêted like filmstars at the end, with the other guests queuing up to get their menus autographed by them.

Reading certainly got its money's worth from the visit of the Prince of Wales, who packed in visits to many of the town's leading employers and other major institutions. He started at Suttons Seeds' trial grounds, where he inspected a guard of honour consisting of 177 ex-servicemen in the employ of the company – conjuring up a wonderful vision of rifle drill being performed with hoes and rakes. Apparently the Prince displayed a keen interest in examples of seeds in process of germination, and in a large model of the firm's premises. He was also greatly interested in the fertilising of gloxinias – happy memories that no doubt sustained him during his long years of exile after abdication.

At Huntley & Palmer, all six thousand members of staff got a chance to see him. There were spontaneous outbreaks of the song 'God bless the Prince of Wales' and the factory hooter blew. In the event that the role of Prince of Wales ceased to be open to him, he was auditioned as a cake-decorator, being shown how to make the Prince of Wales feathers in icing. The results suggested that he should not give up his day job. In the sorting department, he saw how the misshapen biscuits were fed through the special machine that enabled them to be sold as that teatime delicacy of the poor – broken biscuits.

From there he was whisked to Caversham Bridge, where he unveiled a plaque commemorating the fact that he had almost opened the bridge. A barge conveyed him from Caversham Bridge to Reading Bridge, in the course of which he smoked a cigarette and waved to the crowds gathered along either bank. After lunch at the Town Hall, he went on to visit Simonds' Brewery, the Cooperative Bakery (where he was presented with a three-tiered cake, iced with – you guessed – the Prince of Wales feathers), the tinplate works of Huntley Boorne & Stevens, the Royal Berkshire Hospital, Reading School, the University and Palmer Park, where some ten thousand children were performing games, sports and country dancing. Even then, there were still some Reading people left over to cheer him when he returned to the station to catch the 5.25 back to Paddington.

If this were not enough royal excitement for one year, the King and Queen drove into town the very next week to open the Royal Show at Reading. This was a huge agricultural show, one of the biggest in the country since the First World War. It took place on land on the north side of Henley Road, near the junction with Lower Henley Road. The area is now built upon, but for those few days it was the home for many thousands of prize animals and - a sign of the times – parking for 1,200 cars, managed by the Automobile Association, no less. Admission to the show normally ranged from 1s to 5s, but on the day of the royal visit it was raised to 10s. The mayor published an appeal in the newspaper, asking all those whose houses were on the royal route to hang out flags, so that their majesties did not have to suffer the discomfort of looking at the undecorated houses of commoners while processing to the site in their carriage.

THE BIRTH OF THE WHIFF

One aspect of Reading life that the royal visitors most definitely were not exposed to was the Whitley Whiff. Even three-quarters of a century ago

In the event that the role of Prince of Wales ceased to be open to him, he was auditioned as a cake-decorator, being shown how to make the Prince of Wales feathers in icing

the smell from the sewage works in south Reading was a continual source of complaints. Equally familiar were promises that the next piece of technology to be introduced in the works would solve the problem for good. Thus Alderman Parfitt in 1926 was promising irate local residents that once the proposed new system was working there would be absolutely no smell from it. Identical promises were repeated in the press ten years later, and so the story echoed through the years. Part of the problem in 1926 was said to stem from the rubbish dump next door to the sewage works. This, it turned out, was the shared responsibility of three different committees of the Council and was thus beyond the ability of any mortal man to control.

READING'S CRICKETING KING

In the field of sport, a Reading man was the focus of the nation's attention that summer. A.P.F. (Arthur) Howard was born in the town in 1900 and showed his outstanding ability as a cricketer even as a schoolboy. He once made two centuries in a single afternoon, cycling from one cricket match to another between innings. He went on to win a Cambridge Blue, to play for Berkshire and subsequently for Kent. In 1926 he was captain of the England team, which included Jack Hobbs and Wilfred Rhodes, that regained the Ashes from Australia in the Oval test. He went on to captain England seventeen times, including a successful defence of the Ashes in Australia in 1928–29. Reading in the twentieth century has thus had the distinction of producing *two* of those rarest of beings – a successful England cricket captain – for Howard's success was followed by that of Peter May in the 1950s.

1934

FAMINE AND FASCISM

Hitler comes to power in Germany, but in some parts of Reading there is more concern at the appointment of the town's first lady mayor. The Borough Council houses hunger marchers and Reading Rotary Club hosts a Nazi propagandist. Plans are announced for a third Reading bridge and a Caversham bypass. The end of the trams is nigh but Woodley Aerodrome flourishes.

Although the great depression of the 1930s was heralded by the Wall Street Crash of 24 October 1929, Britain felt many of its worst effects during the mid-1930s. By the time of the recession, many of Britain's workers were protected by a compulsory state insurance scheme. However, this barely lifted many of its recipients above the poverty line and people looked to charities or to the Victorian institution of the Poor Law Guardians to help them survive. At this time outdoor relief was costing Reading Council some £850 a week – far more than they had budgeted for.

A lot of people put their faith in the kinds of radical solutions being adopted by governments overseas. In 1933 they saw a Fascist Government take over in Germany, which by 1936 had reduced the number of unemployed from 6,000,000 to 1,600,000, though some of

Heelas' Minster Street premises, pictured in about 1930.

their methods did not bear close scrutiny. Others looked enviously at the absence of unemployment and the superficial appearance of democracy in the Soviet Union. Late in 1933 the case for Fascism found an unusual outlet in Reading, at the quarterly meeting of the Reading and District Free Church Council in Kings Road. Their guest speaker was Dr Ernest Deissman, a native German who worked as an academic in London and who was an unashamed apologist for the Nazi regime. He recalled the harshness of the Treaty of Versailles, which successive German politicians had failed to redress, thereby giving Hitler his chance. As Deissman put it:

Hitler is a man of courage and action, and he has a definite policy which promises escape from the troubles in which the Germans were involved. . . . he has striven to achieve his ideal of a unified Germany, in which class distinctions would be abolished and all classes would work together for the reconstruction of national life.

Anti-semitism is nothing new, but it is passing through a new phase. To understand it aright, it is necessary to understand the part that Jews played in postwar development. Many of them had, by reason of their business skill, prospered when the bulk of German people were suffering, and they had gained great influence in many of the branches of business and commerce, as well as professional life.

It should be realised that the Jews that came into Germany were of a different type to those who came to England or America. Most of the latter, as their names showed, were of German origin and had been influenced by European ideas, but the Jews who migrated to Germany came from the east and a great many of them were imbued with Communistic and Bolshevik notions. Their influence was hostile to the Government, and it was because of these circumstances that it had been deemed necessary to devise stringent measures against them.

It was true that these had resulted in a certain amount of suffering, but it was not so generally known that in many cases regulations were relaxed as, for instance, in the case of the Civil Service, where all Jews who had served in the war retained their posts. As to the teaching profession, most of the Jews who had lost their position were young men who had not attained Professor's Chairs and were only at the beginning of their work.

A good many of the reports published of happenings in Germany were exaggerated, as the newspapers usually concentrated on incidents of violence or extremism and these were not to be regarded as typical. . . . the great bulk of the German people are not mad or foolish, but they had come to the conclusion that the times demanded abnormal measures.

He finished by declaring his belief that the German nation as a whole was behind Hitler.

The chairman of the meeting thanked Dr Deissmann and assured him that, while they might not agree with all that he had said, there was real sympathy with the difficulties of the German people and sincere wishes for the future prosperity of their country.

In similar vein the Reading Rotary Club invited Dr Hans Schirmer to address them on the subject of 'Some positive aspects of the Nazi movement'. He made the sinister military organisations that Hitler was creating sound more like a German version of the Rotary Club:

They have been charged with militarism from the outside, but their stormtroops are really a kind of discipline which means more perhaps to the young German man than to the young English man – bringing all classes together to make sacrifices for their own country. . . . Instead of being a military and political organisation, theirs was first of all a social movement to deal with their internal difficulties. They do not think so much about outside affairs and certainly did not want to conquer more territory for Germany; the disapproval of Europe was not worth the addition of territory.

The vote of thanks for this piece of Nazi propaganda was given by the leading Reading retailer William McIlroy, who was later to serve as Reading's mayor for a large part of the war years.

Others, even in the early 1930s, saw Hitler as a potential enemy. The headmaster of Reading School took advantage of the annual Speech Day to bemoan the lack of popularity of the school's Officer Training Corps. He concluded: 'However much we may regret it, we may have to look to Herr Hitler as the best recruiting sergeant we can get for our OTC.' This provoked a lively correspondence in the letters page between pacifists and those who embraced the values of the OTC, especially for those boys who could not excel at rugby or cricket.

In another, rather obscure, display of anti-fascism, an unemployed labourer, Charles Reeves, was fined five shillings for chalking anti-Nazi slogans on the pavement outside Huntley & Palmer's factory. His reasons for doing so are lost to history, since the magistrates would not allow him to read out his political manifesto when he appeared before them.

TOTALITARIANISM – BRITISH-STYLE
The papers were full of letters arguing the merits of alternative political systems. One reader shared his experience of attending a fascist rally in Reading:

'However much we may regret it, we may have to look to Herr Hitler as the best recruiting sergeant we can get for our OTC'

St Mary's Butts, viewed from the north in 1932. Behind the policeman, Holmes' furniture store awaits demolition to make way for road widening.

May I, through the medium of your paper, point out the futility of fascism. The other evening I attended a meeting held by the local organisation, and went away fully convinced that if fascism ever came to power, nothing but world war would result.

We listened to an unemployed fascist condemn the Public Assistance Committee and the Means Test. He pointed out the ideal state of affairs, but made no attempt whatsoever to tell us how fascism could bring about that state. Indeed, had it not been for a number of youths wearing black shirts, one might have had the impression of being at a meeting of the Labour Party.

The fascists call upon all to recapture the spirit of 1914, and to make England the first country in the world, but if fascists in other countries call upon their people to do the same, what will happen? To put it briefly, every country will try to outdo the others to such an extent that, in the end, we will well and truly recapture the spirit of 1914.

No, my fascist friends, nationalism is of no use; the only remaining remedy for the present state of things is internationalism.

READING HOSTS HUNGER MARCHERS

Political extremism was one of the means by which the unemployed made their protests known to the Government. Hunger marches were another. One such, en route from south Wales and the west country to London, passed through Reading in February 1934. The organisers sought accommodation from the Council and prompted an argument in the Council Chamber. The Council offered them the lairage room at the cattle market, normally used for storing animals. This meant that the four hundred marchers would be sleeping on stone floors in an unheated building during February. Just to add to the 'treating them like cattle' analogy, the Council offered them straw for their bedding. Labour members and the Reading Solidarity Committee did not think this was

PETAL. A sheath line Evening Gown, in shell pink faille, with ruching of self material at shoulder line and hem ... ... 3½gns.

LEAF. A slender Gown in Lace, with Coatee of Georgette and Lace. Lined throughout. In soft blue, and a host of lovely shades. This Gown is of outstanding value ... 3gns.

1933 – No recession for those who could afford these ball gowns.

good enough. They wanted the men to be offered space at the Corn Exchange or even the Town Hall. It was claimed that previous parties of marchers who had been forced to stay in the cattle market had suffered cases of pneumonia as a result.

The protesters were told that there were not enough sanitary conveniences at the Corn Exchange for 400 men and that, when they had allowed a similar group to use it in the past, it has been left in an unsavoury state. Some of the men, it was claimed, were too verminous to enjoy the luxury of a floor at the Town Hall. As for heating, nightwatchmen's braziers would have been too dangerous, what with all that straw in the room. In any event some of the members felt that, with all those men together in the hall, there would be no need for any form of additional heating. And straw? Why, it was more comfortable than feathers! Or so claimed one member of the Council, who clearly had no experience of sleeping on it. So straw bales in the cattle market it was, and members were told afterwards – with almost a note of regret in some quarters, one felt – that not a single case of pneumonia had been reported.

The *Chronicle* ran a feature claiming that the children in the town's schools were healthier and better-nourished than ever, but their optimism was not always borne out by the facts. A voluntary group had been set up to provide allotments for the unemployed, to give them something to fill their time and to supplement their impoverished diet. Those vegetables were sorely needed in many cases. The Reading Tuberculosis Dispensary Care Association reported a significant increase in the number of cases of TB being reported to them, with malnutrition among the long-term unemployed being a complicating factor in a significant number of cases. A new wing had to be built at the Park Isolation Hospital to cope with the upsurge in TB cases.

MADAM MAYOR

Amid all this, Reading was marking a milestone in women's equality by appointing its first woman Mayor, Edith Sutton. She came from the finest of civic pedigrees. A cousin of the Suttons Seeds family, she was the first woman councillor in the entire country, elected as long ago as 1907. Initially an independent, she joined Labour in 1925. She was the daughter of Alfred Sutton, after whom the schools in east Reading were named, and two of her cousins (John Martin Sutton and Leonard Sutton) both served as mayor before her. She had a lifetime's record of voluntary work in education, as well as sports, music and medical voluntary groups, and had been elected Reading's first female alderman.

But not everybody was overjoyed by her appointment. One person described it as 'a sad mistake – you may never have another man as chief magistrate'. Another, possibly in leaden jest, quoted Lord Tennyson's poem 'The Princess' at the mayor-making:

Man for the field and woman for the hearth,
Man for the sword and for the needle she;
Man with the head and woman with the heart,
Man in command and woman to obey;
All else confusion.

Is it my imagination, or has this poem become less popular in recent years?

RINGING THE CHANGES

Reading found itself at the cutting edge of new technology in 1934 when, after five years of planning, a new automatic telephone exchange was introduced in the town. The *Chronicle* explained this marvel of modern science: 'Under the new system the human element will be completely eliminated on local calls, various pitches of tones and buzzing in the receiver indicating when to dial and denoting when the number is engaged or unobtainable.' The new exchange was to be connected to all 3,000 subscribers in Reading, plus 280 in Tilehurst and 120 in Spencers Wood. A team of eighteen men had been specially recruited to call at the homes of every subscriber and train them individually in the operation of the new system.

The emergency services also got improved communications. A network of sixteen emergency call boxes were being set up at key points around the town, to enable policemen and members of the general public to get in touch directly with the police station. Alderman Venner opened the new service by making the first hoax call – summoning a fire engine to Cemetery Junction when there was no fire there for them to put out.

1933 – The King does his patriotic duty for the radio retailers.

COMING SOON – A NEW BRIDGE FOR READING

A town planning committee had been set up in South Oxfordshire in 1928 to collaborate with Reading in planning for the orderly growth of the greater Reading area. There were fears of ribbon development all along the road between Reading and Henley, and of the wooded hillsides of Mapledurham, Whitchurch and Goring becoming suburbanised. The solutions they came up with in the 1930s still sound radical and controversial today. An inquiry, convened to discuss them, had to change its venue from Goring Church Room to Reading Town Hall, so great was the number of protesters wanting to make their views known.

Reading's Borough Surveyor explained their approach to the traffic problem:

In considering the problem of planning the regional area comprising the Borough of Reading and the surrounding districts, one of the most obvious problems which

*Caversham Court, showing how
the house looked before demolition.*

arose is that of the provision of adequate roads. The enormous increase in speed and volume of road traffic in recent years and their certain future increase makes it, in my opinion, imperative to provide a system of ring roads encircling Reading at a sufficient distance from its centre and connecting the various arterial roads, both existing and proposed.

One of these was to start from the Reading–London road, go under the railway and cross the Thames between Sonning and Reading. It would join the Henley Road somewhere near the village of Playhatch and, heading northwards, cross Kiln Road and then Peppard Road, roughly at the northernmost tip of the Borough. Running past the golf course, it would finally join the Woodcote Road, which was being upgraded as a new Reading–Oxford route. This new road was to be built as a parkway, with substantial tree-belts on either side forming a continuous park for the benefit of people living nearby.

In the centre of Caversham, there were also plans for a new road linking Caversham Bridge to the Woodcote Road. The Council had already bought Caversham Court, the mansion designed by the Houses of Parliament architect Pugin for the Simonds family. The house stood on the line of the proposed new road and the Council duly demolished it. Only its gardens remain today.

COME FLY WITH ME . . .
One Reading business that was growing apace was the airfield at Woodley. Set up by Mr C.O. Powis in 1929 with one employee and no hangar, by 1934 it employed 160 people. There was a thriving flying club, where new

enthusiasts could get a trial lesson for just 15s and visiting flyers could stop over. One of their more eccentric visitors at this time was Lord Apsley, a politician who insisted on flying wearing a bowler hat, which he doffed to the control tower during an impromptu flypast. He later crashed in fog near Rickmansworth, fortunately without serious damage to himself or his headgear.

Aircraft manufacture was also booming locally. Late in 1932 Powis had teamed up with a talented young aircraft designer named F.G. Miles. Their new lightweight plane – the Miles Hawk - first flew in April 1933 and within six months it was in full production. Forty models had already been supplied to customers all over the world, and they saw it heralding in a new era in business flying. With a starting price of £450 and a cruising speed of 100mph, Birmingham was just an hour's flight away and Manchester could be reached in two hours. Among the customers for the various Miles aircraft at this time was the transatlantic aviation pioneer Charles Lindbergh.

Reading airfield was set to grow, according to the operators:

It is only recently that internal airlines have been started in England, but during the next three to four years their growth will undoubtedly be rapid. There is in view the formation of a number of central airports to serve sections of the country, and if this materialises, Reading will have a strong claim to selection as an airport serving the south midlands and south of England.

Reading airfield certainly would grow in importance over the next few years, but not for the reasons they imagined. Quite apart from the new demands that the coming war would place on it, it also made the news in a rather lighter vein in 1936. Mr Gwynne Johns, a 26-year-old ironmonger's clerk from Aberystwyth, announced that he would use Reading airfield as his starting point for an attempt on the world record for a freefall parachute descent. He informed the press that he would fly to a height of 20,000 feet, jump out and fall 18,000 feet before opening his chute.

Empire Air Day at Woodley Aerodrome. The aircraft designer F.G. Miles and his family pose in front of an exhibit.

Broad Street, decorated for King George VI's coronation in 1936, as seen from the top of a tram.

We were told that Mr Johns had made almost thirty parachute descents, 'most of them successful' (which immediately begs two questions: 'What is an unsuccessful parachute descent?' and 'can you have more than one of them?'). The record he was trying to beat was 17,000 feet, held by someone pointedly referred to as the late Mr John Tranum. Again we were left wondering – why was Mr Tranum 'late'? Had he made the basic error of starting his 17,000 foot freefall from an altitude of 17,000 feet? Nothing further about Mr Johns' attempt appeared in the *Chronicle* in the next few weeks so we must assume he did not jump that year. It would have been newsworthy, whichever way it turned out.

TROLLEY BUSES

Another mode of transport was in the news in 1934. The Borough Council had been carrying out a radical review of the town's public transport, comparing the merits of petrol buses, diesel buses and trolley buses against their existing tram services. Their conclusions meant that the days of the Reading trams were numbered. Trolley buses came out as the clear favourites:

In the first place, they are electrically driven and electricity has a more stable price and would, of course, be supplied from the Corporation's own electricity undertaking. Secondly, by reason of its construction, the repair and maintenance of a trolley vehicle is a much simpler and cheaper matter than the repair and maintenance of a motor omnibus. Thirdly, a trolley vehicle is a very quiet-running vehicle with quick acceleration. Fourthly, it can be brought alongside the footpath, which makes for efficient and easy loading, whilst the seating arrangements therein are much more suitable than in an omnibus. Fifthly, the vehicle is one that can be kept clean very easily, and its life can be put at ten years at the minimum. Sixthly, trolley vehicles are not subject to the jurisdiction of the Traffic Commissioners and, whilst we do not desire to make a particular point of the fact, the Corporation, in operating a trolley vehicle system, would be masters in their own house.

Pleasure trip on board Queen of the Thames, c. *1930 – and not a bathing costume to be seen.*

So it was that the Council announced plans to replace their trams and most of their motor buses with trolley buses by 1942, at a cost of around £200,000. Some bus routes would have to remain. Lower Caversham, for example, would continue to have a bus service, since it was not possible to run double-decker vehicles under the old Vastern Road railway bridge. Within a week, the first letters started appearing in the paper, complaining of the desecration of some attractive tree-lined street in one part of the town or another by unsightly overhead wires.

MACS IN THE LOCK
At the outbreak of the First World War we heard that not enough was being seen of young people on the river. In 1934 the river authorities felt that, in some cases, the public were seeing rather too much of them:

River Girls and Sunbathing. No Ban by Conservancy
The Thames Conservancy Board has decided not to place a ban on sunbathing along the riverside and in punts and other river craft. Hitherto, the Board's by-laws, which were last revised in 1898, did not deal with such modern innovations. When, therefore, it was decided to frame 53 new by-laws to cope with the modern conditions, the Board took a broad-minded view and demanded that bathers should wear regulation costumes only in the locks.

In an interview an official said: 'The board has always attempted to understand modern conditions. We have no objection to sunbathing, providing it takes place where it does not annoy other people. When boats are crowded together in locks we think the more scantily-attired bathers should have some considerations for their neighbours, and in the locks we have decided to insist on regulation costume, which is what is known as a 'University' costume, over which must be worn a mackintosh or coat. The Board intend to prosecute bathers who wear only shorts.'

1939

GOODBYE TRAMS, HELLO MR HITLER

The lights go out all over Europe – except in Reading, where the Co-op Jam Factory fire illuminates the night sky for miles around; and, as Reading prepares for war, Shirley Temple packs them in at the Vaudeville Cinema, playing 'The Little Princess'.

The trams had been part of the life of Reading for well over thirty years, but by the 1930s they had been overtaken by the growth in the town's traffic. Or, to be more precise, part of the problem was that the growing traffic could not overtake them, as they trundled sedately down the middle of the road. Motor buses had started to appear after the First World War and, as we have heard, trolley buses began to replace the trams from 1935. By 20 May 1939 they were ready to run their last service. The *Chronicle* looked back on their career:

Saturday saw in Reading the last of the electric tramcars, which served the town so well for thirty-six years, and on Sunday trolley buses took their place on the main route. Those who can recall the old horse-trams, when an extra horse was put on at Factory Bridge to assist with the load there, will recognise the more fully the advance made in public transport. The comfort, smooth running and speed of the trolley buses are greatly appreciated, and not the least advantage is that the user is not set down in the middle of a busy road to risk his life from several lines of traffic. Motorists will also benefit from the removal of highly obstructive vehicles.

The only drawback is the loss of the open upper decks of the trams, which afforded welcome fresh air facilities to thousands of people, especially in sultry weather. Much interest is being centred in the solution of the problem of Elm Park concentration. It is well known that as many as 120 people, if not more, have been packed upon a tram at certain exceptional times during the football season, but in the case of the buses it is not usual to allow more than five people beyond the seating capacity, and no standing upstairs. It is obvious that Reading will require a substantial quantity of rolling stock to deal with these emergencies. . . .

In a few years' time an electric tram running on rails will be as rare a sight in England as is a hansom cab. But the

May 1939, and the Mayor guides the last tram home.

Station Hill, viewed from the east, showing construction in progress on the south side of the street in the late 1930s. The area beneath the viaduct they were building would serve as air raid shelters.

system has conferred a great boon. Trams have, in the Borough, run 12,500,000 miles. Some 155 million passengers have been carried, earning total receipts of nearly £2 million. The electric trams have contributed to the rates the net figure of £39,000. Will the trolley buses do as well? A great deal depends on the public, though nationally applied burdens have made the running of transport schemes expensive.

As with their opening, the last tram was driven by members of the Council. Only councillors and Council officials were allowed to ride on it, much to the disappointment of the large crowds that turned up to see it off. Special commemorative tickets were issued and the tram set off down the Oxford Road. It was pursued by a gaggle of about fifty cyclists, who wove suicidally around it like mice under the feet of an elephant. Behind it, the queue of frustrated traffic built up steadily to about half a mile in length. Mayor McIlroy took the controls for the last section of the journey through the town centre, where the crowds sang 'Auld Lang Syne'. The band who were playing at the Ship Hotel that day turned out to serenade it, as it turned into Duke Street for the last time.

At the depot the mayor, for some reason clutching a large spanner, proposed a toast to the transport service. Many of those who had attended the launch of the trams in 1903 were dead, but Alderman Bale could remember riding on the old horse-drawn trams, had ridden the first electric tram (for which he still had the commemorative ticket) and had lived to see their closure.

The introduction of the new trolley buses was not entirely without incident. They suffered initially from a nasty case of sticking horns. Drivers were left to wrestle with them, as shoppers came out into the street to see what all the noise was all about, and gaggles of small boys

August 1939 – The Co-op advertise in the very week the factory burnt down.

congregated to offer deeply unhelpful advice. In one case, the driver, conductor and two inspectors had to dismantle the entire horn assembly to restore peace to the neighbourhood.

But the main preoccupation of the town was the preparation for war. You can read a full account of the war years in Reading in my book *Reading at War*. In the remainder of this chapter, we will look at the last days of peace in the town.

FLAMING MINCEMEAT!

The emergency services got some practice for any blazes that might lay ahead, when one of the buildings at the CWS Jam Factory in Coley caught fire. A thousand barrels of mincemeat (a product whose incendiary qualities are not always fully appreciated) and a lorry went up in flames:

Hundreds of people who witnessed the blaze from the banks of the River Kennet were thrilled by the gallant efforts of the Reading Fire Brigade, the Auxiliary Fire Service and the Works Fire Brigade in preventing the flames from spreading to the main manufactory. In half an hour, flames which sometimes leapt nearly a hundred feet high had razed the building to the ground. So fierce were these flames that windows in the adjacent Peel Preserve department were destroyed, whilst the district was lit up for miles around. . . . The cause of the outbreak is at present a mystery.

PREPARING FOR WAR

Nobody was betting against a war by now; even the Salvation Army was mobilising. They bought Rosehill at Emmer Green, the house which until 1938 had served as a preparatory school for the Oratory School. Their plans were to decant their national headquarters staff there, if and when war broke out. The Council announced plans to spend between £40,000 and £50,000 on building air raid shelters for the town's schoolchildren, and the area under the viaduct then being constructed at Station Approach was also to be adapted to provide shelters.

Local employers were making their own preparations. Thorneycrofts of Caversham were building five shelters, each capable of holding sixty people, at a cost of £1200. They were to be lit by battery-powered lights, on the assumption that no air raid would last longer than fifteen minutes. Pulsometer carried out tests to see how quickly they could evacuate their factory, and were pleased to find that all their 700 staff were in their safety trenches within three minutes. They were also training up their own, fully equipped decontamination squad, to deal with incendiary or gas attacks.

One aspect of the war – the never-ending stream of good advice from the Government and other quarters – was already under way. The Co-op were rather prematurely distributing a leaflet entitled 'Your food in wartime', and their advertisements in the press advised customers on the best products for storing (or hoarding, as it became known in the war – with substantial fines attached). The authorities were not helped by bogus ARP wardens going from door to door, trying to persuade housewives to buy up stocks of certain proprietary brands of foodstuffs.

The real ARPs were also getting into practice. They ran an exercise, in the course of which a house in Dover Street was deemed to have been destroyed by a bomb, a gas main at the Argyle Street/Argyle Road junction was supposed to be fractured, more bombs had allegedly fallen on the Tilehurst Road/Belle Vue Road junction, there were imaginary incendiaries and casualties at the Tilehurst Road/Prospect Street junction, an invisible bomb crater at Castle Hill and other fictitious incidents in Coley Place and St Mary's Butts. In short, they dealt with rather more widespread imaginary damage than was sustained in Reading during any one raid in the real war – with one notable exception. About 300 volunteers took part in the exercise. As part of it, householders were encouraged to install blackout curtains to their own houses, much to the delight of local drapers. Military planes flew over the town, to see how effective the blackout was. There was a problem, though: the railways did not co-operate with the exercise, keeping the lights in their goods yards shining brightly. The pilots apparently mistook these for the street lights in the town centre.

Commander Hassard Short, the town's leading ARP officer, none the less waxed optimistic about the exercise: 'So far as we could observe from

'So fierce were these flames that windows in the adjacent Peel Preserve department were destroyed, whilst the district was lit up for miles around'

the ground, the blackout itself was very effective – definitely better than the previous one – and we understand that aeroplane observers had great difficulty in locating certain targets.' A blackout that is effective from the ground is all very well, but who has ever been bombed by a plane travelling along the ground? And if the aeroplane observers had difficulty locating certain targets, it was probably because they were dazzled by the lights from the railway yards.

The ARP authorities also advised their audiences that respirators and anti-gas helmets for children would be distributed in a month or two. They would be too late for the outbreak of hostilities but, as we now know, the only casualties resulting from a gas attack in Reading in the whole of the war were caused by our own side! The correct use of gasmasks was a matter of widespread concern among the local populace, not least among those who wanted to know how to wear them with spectacles (wearing the spectacles over the gasmask was not recommended). There was also the problem of the eyepieces steaming up; people were told to rub them with soap to prevent this happening.

In the last week of August 1939, Reading was designated a 'specified area' – that is to say, one which was officially regarded as being in danger of being bombed. The brighter side of this, always assuming one was insanely optimistic enough to see a bright side, was that the town was supplied earlier with all the necessary accessories for being bombed, such as Anderson shelters. By the end of the month war preparations were in full swing – the Territorials and the anti-aircraft crews were being called up; the first instructions for masking car headlamps in the blackout were being published, and controls on the use of factory sirens for anything other than air raid warnings were in preparation.

EXPEDITIONARY FARCE

But not everybody had their eye on the war in August 1939. Two pupils from Reading and Leighton Park Schools announced their intention to cycle across France to Geneva. They were planning to leave in mid-August, and spend twenty-four days covering 1,610 miles (they were going the scenic way, rather than the most direct). One of the pupils, Gerald Smallcombe, explained that, since he was interested in improved international relations, he was particularly looking forward to seeing the famous meeting place of the League of Nations. This must

1939 – Shirley helps us forget the imminent war.

qualify as some kind of record, as the worst possible time ever to visit eastern France to study improved international relations. A little while later and they would have been coming home via Dunkirk, with the troops.

ESCAPE WITH SHIRLEY

But for those looking to get away from it all in August 1939, it had to be the cinema. They were showing Shirley Temple in 'The Little Princess'. In this Frances Hodgson Burnett story, Shirley, now a seasoned performer of nine years old, 'acts with more conscious skill and more perception of the emotional demands of her part than ever before.' (Perhaps we can hope that Arnold Schwarzenegger is just a late developer.) Shirley played a child at a boarding school who is reduced to penury when her father is reported dead, and is turned into a drudge by her wicked headmistress. It takes the intervention of Queen Victoria, no less, who was making a visit nearby, to rescue her. Of course, her father turns out to be not dead at all – he had probably just gone into hiding until she grew out of simpering. Just the sort of film to make being bombed by the Luftwaffe seem like an attractive alternative.

FREEZE AND FLOODS   1947

Britain – and Reading – suffer the worst freeze and flooding of the century – large parts of Caversham are cut off. The town's University announces its move to the Whiteknights estate.

January and February 1947 brought some of the coldest weather that Reading had seen for many years. Minus 12 degrees Centigrade was recorded on the Woodcote Road. The toboggans came out in Prospect Park and there was skating on Whiteknights Lake and other stretches of water, until snow covered the ice too deeply.

The Government's austerity plans for fuel supplies could not cope with the weather. There was not enough coal to go round and what there was could not be delivered through the ice and snow. The Government announced that there would have to be 50 per cent cuts in the fuel allocations to industry. Thousands of jobs in Reading were threatened by the decision and a Fuel Allocations Committee sat in daily session to hear pleas from local firms who needed more coal. Nobody escaped. Even those who relied upon gas or electricity faced unpredictable power cuts, since the coal could not reach the power stations or the gasworks. Ingenuity was the order of the day. Berkshire Printing operated some of its presses by hand and redeployed other staff on cleaning duties. Ancient stand-by generating equipment at the Huntley & Palmer factory was hurriedly serviced and brought back into use. At the Miles aircraft factory at Woodley, winches, tractors and ex-ARP trailer pumps were hitched up to generators to provide power. Some rooms were even lit by car headlights.

Broad Street, looking west, 1947.

Flood scenes around Reading, March 1947.

No area of activity was spared from the cuts. Shop displays were lit by paraffin lamps and candles; dentists did their work using foot-powered drills; police officers blundered around in a police station lit only by a few oil lamps. Even Simonds' Brewery was reduced to making mini-brews, just to keep their yeast alive, and a shortage of beer was forecast for Easter. But no alternative could be found to electricity for the hare at Reading greyhound stadium and the race meetings were cancelled. Only one enterprise flourished: there was standing room only in the reading room of

the Library, as laid-off workers looked for somewhere to keep themselves warm and occupied.

Elsewhere, the illumination of the Town Hall clock was switched off and pianos replaced organs for church services. Accumulator batteries for radios, which had hitherto taken two days to recharge, now took five as a result of all the power cuts. In Zinzan Street, a 79-year-old woman, reading by the light of two candles propped on the arms of her chair, set fire to herself and died from the burns.

There was an upsurge of public opinion against a Government which, some felt, had got them into this situation, and graffiti along the lines of 'socialism = no warmth, no jobs and no hope' began appearing on walls. Reading's Labour MP Ian Mikardo had his own explanation of the fuel crisis, tracing it back to 1913 and the private pit-owners' unwillingness to invest in their mines, which had subsequently closed a thousand pits and put half a million miners out of jobs.

The thaw, when it came, was unexpectedly swift but the results were predictably disastrous. The ground was still frozen, preventing the water from draining into the soil. This was how the *Chronicle* recorded events, one week in March:

Most Serious Floods Since 1894. Water in Houses and Roads Inundated

The rapid thaw, which followed the recent severe weather, produced the most serious floods experienced in the life of most people in the Thames Valley. All along the river, there are vast areas under water and thousands of people have been forced to live in the top rooms of their houses because the ground floor has been flooded – to a depth of several feet in some cases. From Saturday onwards, the River Thames at Reading has been several feet above normal, though not quite so high as in the record-breaking floods of 1894. The various tributaries have also overflowed their banks, to add to the devastation.

Practically the whole of lower Caversham has been flooded; many roads are under water and people have had to be evacuated from their homes. At one time the area was threatened with isolation from the remainder of Reading but, fortunately, the level of the floods has not risen, as was feared, during the week.

The floods arrived with unexpected rapidity during Friday night, when the river rose by fifteen inches in a few hours, and by Monday the river at Caversham was four feet above its normal level. This was then six inches below the level recorded in the great floods of 1894, the highest known;

The buses tried to cope with conditions more suited to gondolas.

*Caversham housewives wade down
to the shops.*

but even this level was exceeded along some reaches of the Thames during the week.

The course of the river has completely disappeared in most parts of Reading district and in its place there is one gigantic stretch of turbulent water bounded on the south by the railway embankment and on the north by the Warren, South View Avenue and Lower Henley Road. De Montfort Island has completely disappeared, the tops of trees being the only indication of its position, while Caversham Lock and the Clappers footpath are under water, the lock-keeper's house being approached by a bridge of barges.

The seriousness of the position was brought home to the people of the town on Saturday, when broadcast instructions were given that all drinking water should be boiled before use. . . . For several days the Fobney and Southcote waterworks has been isolated, the only method of approach being by boat, and the level of the water is now higher than that of the works. In spite of the fact that all available staff have been sandbagging the filter beds to keep out the flood water there has been no means of being sure that the flood water had not by-passed the filters. All the water is being heavily chlorinated and samples which have been taken daily in the area have so far shown the water to be safe.

An urgent request to reduce consumption has not been followed for, surprising as it may seem, consumption has risen in the past few days. . . . Because of the high level of the river, the undertaking's turbines have stopped and the works are running to full capacity on auxiliary power. The works are heavily overloaded and consumption must be reduced if the supply of water is to be maintained. . . .

Some thousands of families are confined to the upper floors of their houses and about two hundred people, mostly the aged and infirm or sick, have been evacuated either to relatives or friends, or to Battle Hospital. Altogether 1,600 houses are affected by flood water and the majority of these are in the area of Caversham bounded by Westfield Road, South View Avenue, Star Road and the river. In some places the water lies in the ground floor rooms three feet deep.

A service of lorries, and boats supplied and manned by the Thames Conservancy, takes workers and shoppers from their flooded homes to a point where they can reach the public transport, and tickets enabling the holders to

The indomitable ladies of the WVS arrive with their tea urn.

obtain hot meals at Civic restaurants are issued to residents in the flooded area. Members of the WVS . . . have been touring the district supplying hot meals and drinks to those who are unable to leave their homes. During Tuesday afternoon two amphibious vehicles, loaned by the army, arrived and have been used to carry workers and shoppers to dry land, and tradesmen to deliver their goods.

An enormous problem has been that of sanitation and refuse collections have been made twice daily in the Caversham area, while people in the district have been warned by loudspeakers of the danger of throwing refuse and dirty water into the floods because of the danger to health. Only by the strictest attention to cleanliness will disease be averted.

By considerable ingenuity and resourcefulness, the deliveries of essential goods such as milk, groceries and bread has been kept going. . . . The longest period where anyone has been without a delivery of these essential items has been one day. Between Friday night and Monday morning the postal authorities found it impossible to deliver telegrams, parcels and letters in Lower Caversham, but on Monday morning an Assistant Inspector volunteered to attempt delivery. Driving a large van he succeeded, after several unsuccessful efforts, in delivering almost all his letters and telegrams, some of them having to be offered to householders at the end of a long pole held by a postman in a punt.

In spite of the cattle market being covered in several inches of water, cattle sales were being held as arranged, beasts and buyers paddling around in the flood water.

At the weekend, all telephone subscribers in Caversham were cut off from Reading and all other parts of the country because flood water had entered a telephone cable connecting the Reading and Caversham exchanges. . . . With the help of a Corporation electricity repair wagon, Post Office engineers were able on Monday to sling overhead cables over Caversham Bridge to restore a restricted service to the two parts of the town. Calls from Reading to Caversham had to be made via the operator and were restricted to six minutes only.

The floods recede and the clean-up begins.

Life was disrupted in all sorts of other ways. Only one of the Council schools in Caversham was open; Sonning was completely cut off from Oxfordshire; for the first time since its establishment in 1880, the Reading and Caversham Laundry on George Street had to close, after the water entered its boilers, and yet again the greyhound racing, which in those days took place at a stadium near the Norcot roundabout, had to be cancelled. This time, the hare had drowned.

By the following Monday, most of the floods had subsided and homeowners could begin to assess the damage. All their floor coverings were ruined, and there was a coating of slime that had to be scrubbed off the floorboards. Most people were able to rekindle their wartime stoicism in the face of adversity, but the biggest grumble concerned the extra fuel allocation given them by the Government to dry out their saturated homes. Just a quarter of a hundredweight of coal was hopelessly inadequate, and even that had to be fetched by the householder from the depot – they even had to supply their own sack! At least each householder received a bar of soap from a Hardship Fund set up by the Mayor of Reading. The public were warned against bogus collectors for the Fund who were doing the rounds, and were told to give only to those with properly printed labels on their tins.

Outside, the streets needed to be hosed down to remove their coating of mud. As the river returned to its normal course, further evidence of the power of the floods could be seen. Huge amounts of heavy debris had been washed into the weir and workers had the difficult and dangerous job of fishing it out before it did any further damage. The water had also dug a deep channel along the towpath, by-passing the weir gates completely.

Flooding became a political issue. Reading MP Ian Mikardo and the local Conservative candidate for the Abbey ward both visited victims, and the Communist parties throughout the Thames Valley convened a conference in order to advise the authorities on the correct socialist response to the disaster.

UNIVERSITY MOVES TO WHITEKNIGHTS

In the midst of all this, the University announced that it would be leaving London Road, where it had been based since 1906. They had bought the 300 acre Whiteknights estate for an undisclosed sum, and would soon begin the lengthy process of decanting from London Road. Whiteknights, they said, 'would provide room for expansion to any extent which might hereafter reasonably be desired'.

The estate had a long history. The white knight in its name was said to be Gilbert de Montalieu, a close friend of William the Conqueror. The Catholic Englefield family later owned it from the sixteenth to the eighteenth centuries. There was a slight interruption to their ownership in 1558, when Sir Francis Englefield was forced to flee the country as the Protestant Queen Elizabeth ascended to the throne. His lands were forfeit to the Crown in 1585, but the family was able to buy them back again in 1606 after Elizabeth's death. From 1798 the estate was owned by the Marquis of Blandford, whose lavish spending (among other things, on the landscaping of the grounds) had bankrupted him by the time he succeeded to the title of Duke of Marlborough. Later owners included Lord Hurst, founder of the General Electric Company.

The University itself had grown apace since making the transition from a University College in 1926. Its student numbers had risen from 693 in 1944/45 to over 900 in 1947 and priority was being given to the needs of former servicemen who had missed out on further education as a result of the war.

KOOL KATS, BLACK SHEEP AND THE PALACE

1961

Britain sees the introduction of betting shops. The Palace Theatre – one of Reading's best known entertainment venues – closes. Reading's post-war office boom begins and early office automation heralds the computer age. Race relations show signs of tension.

The idea that teenagers were merely adults with squeaky voices had well and truly disappeared by 1961. They commanded a great deal of spending power and attempts were being made to cater for their unique entertainment requirements in all sorts of ways. One of the more radical (and controversial) of these was a prototype scheme set up in Reading and intended as a model for similar clubs nationwide. The Kool Kat Club at Coronation Square, Southcote, was built by Reading Borough Council and leased for a nominal sum to an organisation called Youth Venture. Their aim was to attract the non-joiners of normal club life – the

Broad Street, viewed from the east, from the junction with Cross Street, 1960.

'Untouchables', as someone rather slightingly referred to them – into some form of organised recreation. It had everything an untouchable (sorry, non-joiner) might want of a club – juke box, dance hall, television room and coffee bar.

Local residents were not best pleased at having this facility on their doorsteps and argued that the premises could be better used by those living in the area. None the less, the club had a high profile opening. Five hundred teenagers turned up to see Vince Eager, the resident star of BBC television's pop programme 'Drumbeat', do the honours. (It was supposed to have been Tommy Steele, but he was unavailable on the night.) The Council's 'hip' credentials were entrusted to Alderman Busby, who said: 'I am sure we have created today in Reading something we are going to be proud of for many years to come, and something that will be followed up and down the country.' His optimism was ill-founded. Within three months the club was closed, the victim of what were described as a series of acts of violence on the part of a small minority of its 220 members. Even after its demise, a mother gave evidence in court that it was the evil influence of the Kool Kat Club that led her seventeen-year-old son off the straight and narrow and into stealing cars.

Friar Street, north side in 1961 – soon to be redeveloped with Friar's Walk shopping arcade.

Cars like this 1961 Ford Popular enabled many more families to join the motoring classes.

Another rather grander and longer established place of entertainment met its demise at about the same time. The Palace Theatre in Cheapside (next to the Odeon Cinema) had been built by a consortium of local businessmen in 1907. One writer on Reading, Alan Wykes, described it thus: 'It was a fine example of the Edwardian music hall. Its plush and gilt, abundant cupids, mahogany bars and bosomy barmaids were typical of the provincial variety theatre.'

For over forty years it thrived, attracting many top names to the town. But by the 1950s the competition from the cinemas and, more particularly, the television was beginning to tell. The programmes went steadily down-market, bringing in 'Believe it or Not'-type freak shows and seedy sex revues. Among the less edifying productions on offer during this period were 'Lester's Midgets – 20 living doll people, including the smallest man alive – 2ft 6in Henry Behrens – in a miniature music hall' and 'We Couldn't Wear Less – featuring the latest rage from the American strip shows, the Wriggle Dance'. But even this wholesome fare could not sustain them financially. By the late 1950s, the Palace began to close sporadically. One of the last acts to make an appearance there – and certainly the last to provoke his audience to riot – was an eighteen-year-old rock and roller called Cliff Richard.

Christmas 1959 saw the Theatre brought out of retirement to stage its 29th and last pantomime – a two-week run of 'Babes in the

The Palace Theatre opened on Cheapside in 1907, and succumbed to one of Reading's office building booms in 1961.

Wood'. This time, it was not another of their sleazy revues: the babes were of the infant variety. There was wild talk for a time of the Council taking over The Palace, but it finally went the way of so many other Reading buildings in the 1960s – sold to a property speculator, to be redeveloped for offices in 1961.

New technology was starting to make its presence felt in the town. After an audit of their payroll arrangements, the Council decided to introduce three special accounting machines, at a cost of £2,837 14s each, that would enable them to reduce their payroll staff from thirty-four to twenty-seven. Councillor Stoddart urged the Finance Committee to be very careful of this new machine accounting. He had known of empires being built around machines that could achieve the very opposite of what was desired. Before you knew it, there would be insufficient staff to operate the machines and more would have to be recruited.

As if to symbolise the changes that were taking place in Reading's economy, the ironworks by Reading Bridge – a long-standing eyesore – were to be replaced by a ten-storey office block, the building which we now know as Reading Bridge House. But there were fears that this huge block would be over-dominant in its location and would add to traffic congestion locally. Its supporters were, however, persuaded by the argument that it would employ no more people than the ironworks itself. If this were true, the ironworks staff must have been so tightly packed with workers that there would have been no room to swing a hammer.

1968   MULTI-RACIAL READING

Nationwide and in Reading, race relations reach crisis point in the wake of Enoch Powell's 'Rivers of Blood' speech. We get our first taste of decimal currency. A revolution in the town's retailing begins and there is a promise of an end to Reading's traffic misery. The last trolley bus runs and the first multi-storey car park opens.

Reading has been a multi-racial community for many years. In 1956 a black journalist came to the town and found that he suffered less racial antagonism here than in many other places he had visited. His standards were admittedly modest: he judged Reading in terms of whether the shopkeepers refused point-blank to serve him, whether landlords took coloured tenants and by the number of jobs that were open to people like him. At that time, there were an estimated 250 West Indians in the town and their numbers were predicted to double within the year. The Asian population was also on the increase. By 1968 the number of youngsters unable to speak English was large enough to warrant special action by the education authority:

Children who cannot speak English
The problem in Reading of children who cannot speak English has increased so rapidly that a special reception centre is to be set up so they can be given a concentrated course in the English language. The centre will be based at the Alfred Sutton Boys' School annexe and it will open in September. . . . It was estimated that when the centre opened there would be about fifty non-English speaking pupils in attendance. . . . It is not intended that any child should be full-time at the centre because of special problems. They will spend some time at the school where they will eventually be pupils. As their knowledge of English progresses, they will spend more time at school and less at the centre.

By the time the centre opened, its numbers had already grown to seventy, and included Chinese, Portuguese and Pakistani children among others. But even before it even opened, it began to look as if Reading could suddenly become a whole lot more multi-cultural:

Reading authorities will not be stampeded into any precipitate action if the town is faced with a sudden influx of Asian immigrants from Kenya, Malawi or any other newly independent African state. The authorities feel that the Government's emergency 'flood barrier' against Asians from Kenya or elsewhere with British passports will meet the circumstances. . . .

After stressing the town's history of good race relations, the authorities pointed out that Reading did not have problems of the magnitude of Bradford, Birmingham or Wolverhampton. A spokesman for the Ministry of Labour said:

There is no colour bar in this town and the chances are that if the Ministry advertised for a cleaner the applicant would be coloured. . . . Furthermore, . . . Reading had one of the lowest unemployment percentages in the country. At the beginning of February there were 1,400 job vacancies and 1,300 men, women and school-leavers unemployed. . . . The Ministry spokesman said that if the new Asian immigrants found their way to Reading they would be 'snapped up like hot cakes'. This was because both the Indians and Pakistanis from East Africa were more technically qualified than other coloured immigrants from other parts of the world. . . .

The authorities agreed that Reading's one danger spot in catering for the new coloured immigrants was housing. The Council was aware that there was not nearly enough housing in the town for white families, let alone coloured immigrant families. The position was not good, but it was not as bad as that in other towns. . . .

The one thing feared by the authorities, and the representatives of the various political parties, is that the arrival of the immigrants will become a red-hot racial issue.

'There is no colour bar in this town and the chances are that if the Ministry advertised for a cleaner the applicant would be coloured'

MR. DINE SAYS:

'Have fun tonight-cook your own Barbecue!'

It's new; it's different! Come and 'Barbecue Dine' in attractive open air surroundings. We supply the food; you prepare it just as you like it.

Choose from:

Steak 3/6   Baked Jacket
Gammon 3/6   Potatoes 1/-
Lamb Cutlets 3/6   Coleslaw Salad 1/-
Sausages 2/6   Raw Tomatoes 6d.

GROSVENOR HOUSE

Kidmore Road, Caversham. Berks. Tel: ORE4 72045.

drop anchor where you see this sign

Anchor Hotels & Taverns Ltd.

1968 – Reading is introduced to the novelty of the barbecue, except here you buy the food from the pub and cook it yourself on their barbecue.

In April a body called the Reading Association for Racial Harmony announced its intention to set up a multi-racial liaison committee in the town, and called a public meeting to discuss it. In the *Chronicle*'s view, such a body was not needed. The town's several thousand immigrants had generally blended happily with the rest of the population.

They could not have picked a worse week to call their meeting. A few days before it, Enoch Powell made his notorious 'rivers of blood' speech and was sacked by Edward Heath. In the local papers there were pro-Powellite letters, calling for immigration bans and repatriation, the South Oxfordshire Conservative Association passed resolutions along much the same lines and two Conservative members of Earley Parish Council quit the party in support of Powell and formed a local branch of the National Front. Building workers on a site at the Royal Berkshire Hospital walked off the job in support of Powell's views. The Reading Trades Council proposed a motion of censure of their action and themselves split over the issue. One of their members was reported as saying: 'I am not prepared to condemn all the people who did walk off that site as racialists. There is a frightening degree of racialism in the town. People do have general fears and anxieties. It is no good condemning them all as racialists. It is not going to solve the problem.'

Thus, over 250 people packed into the racial harmony meeting at Kendrick School, and it soon became clear that not everybody was happy with the principle of the Association or with the way it was being organised. As one black member of the audience put it: 'What gives you white intellectuals the right to set up a committee without the backing of the working man or the mass of the coloured community in this town?' Another immigrant asked: 'The Indian is alien to the West Indian, the Pakistani to the Indian and the African to them all, so how do we integrate?'

Mr James Ifill, the organiser of something called the Cosmopolitan Club, denounced the new committee and claimed that his organisation was already fulfilling its function. Others warned that the new body would bear a heavy burden of responsibility if it became a focus for racial discord. In the midst of this sat the unfortunate Bishop of Reading, the Revd Eric Knell, who had been lumbered with the job of chairing the proceedings. The meeting eventually agreed to give the new body a trial period.

In the months that followed Reading was visited by a number of speakers who added fuel to any flames of racial tension that might be burning in the town. Conservative MP John Biggs-Davison, the Member for Chigwell, called for a ban on immigration while speaking at the Gerry Vaughan Luncheon Club. He did so in the nicest possible way, of course: 'All must be treated equally who are here, but now we must put up the "house full" sign.'

Enoch Powell himself came to address the Reading University Conservative Association. The police imposed maximum security, since a similar engagement at Exeter the same week had ended in a riot. Stewards tried to limit admissions to bona fide members of their association, but enough infiltrators got in to make for a frisky meeting, no doubt roared on by the thousand or so demonstrators assembled outside. But Powell at least got the chance to finish his speech on this occasion.

A rather different point of view was put forward to the University in November by one Michael Abdul Malik – better known as the Black Power advocate Malcolm X. He had previously given a talk at the Rainbow Hall in Reading and expressed his views so robustly that he was sent to prison for them. His first multi-racial engagement after his release was to speak at Reading University to their branch of the United Nations Student Association. He emphasised the points in his talk by waving a switchblade knife around and called one of his fellow-speakers (a Labour MP) a racist for referring to 'second generation immigrants'. He also offered the following heart-warming sentiment: 'Anyone who calls himself white is a racialist. He is dirty. My aim is to wipe out white people.' One of his fellow-speakers likened him to the white supremacists of South Africa.

Malcolm X had previously given a talk at the Rainbow Hall in Reading and expressed his views so robustly that he was sent to prison for them

NEW WAYS OF SHOPPING

The retail industry was also changing. Great Western Motors on Wokingham Road became one of the first petrol-filling stations in the country to go self-service. The *Chronicle* printed detailed advice on what to do, for the benefit of the bewildered: 'No one need feel apprehensive about their first visit', the management reassured us – and customers were lured by the promise of quadruple Green Shield trading stamps in return for filling up themselves, so to speak. They even employed a member of staff to patrol the forecourt, looking for customers whose mechanical knowledge did not extend to removing the petrol cap, as well as attending to their other needs, such as oil, water and air.

Among their customers' other needs may well have been an explanation of the money in their pockets, for this was the year that the British public got its first sight of decimal coinage. The first 5p and 10p coins were introduced in April and a *Chronicle* reporter went on to the streets to test the preparedness of the Reading public. One shopkeeper refused point-blank to accept this toy money, and others displayed varying degrees of confusion. A bus conductor pleaded with the reporter to pay his fare in proper money if at all possible; the lady behind the counter in Woolworths had to call her supervisor to assist with the transaction; one old fellow

Baylis' supermarket, pictured just before its move from the corner of Broad Street and St Mary's Butts in 1968.

told him his coin was a rarity (a mere 35 million had been issued that first day) and advised him to hoard it, while others explained patiently that 10p was not the equivalent in value to the old ten shillings. All this was before the full introduction of decimal coinage in 1971.

In the high street we could see the beginning of the departure of mainstream food shopping from the town centre. Baylis the grocers announced that they were to sell off their supermarket site on the corner of Broad Street and St Mary's Butts. They had traded from there since 1875, but were now going to concentrate on more suburban locations, such as Shinfield, Tilehurst and Caversham. They blamed their move partly on the lack of car parking in the town centre. Baylis's Broad Street rivals David Grieg were installing closed-circuit television. Their Reading branch was the first outside central London to be accorded this dubious distinction, but it was not because they had a particular local problem with thieves. There had only ever been four prosecutions for shoplifting from the Reading branch. The aim seemed rather to be to rely on their deterrent value.

But an even more radical change was afoot on the retail front. Recognise this?

A covered commercial centre spread over four acres of ground, with car parks, restaurants, cinemas, lifts and escalators. . . . Ninety shops of varying sizes, offering a

The Butts commercial centre. Artist's impression as seen from above on the north side of the Oxford Road, c. 1970.

well-balanced selection of consumer goods . . . air conditioning and a fine weather promenade . . . a place where a housewife can do her shopping in comfort without getting wet or having her hairdo spoiled in high wind – that is what Reading will have early in 1971. It has been the dream of Reading Borough Council for more than a decade. Now the green light has been switched on and work will commence on January 1.

It started life as the Butts Centre and was later reborn as the Broad Street Mall. Built at a cost to the developer of £3 million, it also held out the promise of £200,000 a year in rent and rates to the Council. One of its

Finch's Buildings, on the south side of Hosier Street, 1957. They were demolished to make way for the Civic Centre complex.

more unusual proposed features was to be a cloakroom, where visitors from the country could deposit their galoshes and outdoor coats before setting off round the centre in comfort. No mention was made of where they could tie the horse.

Like so many Reading projects this one was also a long time in the making. Reading had first brought in consultants in 1959 to help develop what was then just the germ of an idea. The site, at the junction of Oxford Road and St Mary's Butts, was chosen in 1962 and bought by compulsory purchase in 1964.

PLENTY OF JAMS TODAY . . .

Reading's traffic problem was certainly a deterrent to anyone thinking of travelling into town. Questions were asked about it in Parliament, bringing the glad news that the Reading bypass (more generally known as the M4 motorway) was due to begin construction in 1969. This was not before time, as far as some of the long-suffering residents of inner Reading were concerned. In those days long-distance east–west traffic threaded its way through the centre of town, along Crown Street, Pell Street and Berkeley Avenue. The residents even got up a petition to try to hurry up the construction of the motorway. Easter 1968, which for once was marked by good weather, illustrated the scale of the problem. Holiday

Chatham Street car park, 1968.

traffic was queued eastwards out of the town as far as the Wee Waif at Twyford until 9 p.m. on the previous Thursday night. On Monday the queue stretched the other way out of the town, 6 miles back to Theale. It was taking motorists an hour and a half to get through Reading, and they were still queuing in the early hours of Tuesday morning. Government figures showed that the A4 between Reading and Maidenhead was carrying 33,000 vehicles a day, although it had been designed for 11,000 or, at the very most, 15,000. The motorway was urgently needed, not least to reduce the twenty-seven fatalities that occurred in less than a year along the Berkshire section of the A4.

One form of transport that would not be seen on Reading's roads for much longer was the trolley bus, whose final trip was set for 3 November 1968. For weeks beforehand, the trolley buses carried posters reading 'Goodbye' on their sides, and on their penultimate weekend the network was hired out to enthusiasts. One of them even brought over a Belfast trolley bus to run on the network. They had been in service for thirty-two years and had been a particular godsend in wartime, when petrol rationing had led to restricted services on other forms of public transport. Many of the vehicles still had an 'honesty box' for uncollected fares, dating from the wartime years when the vehicles were grossly overcrowded and conductors could not get round to collect all the fares. But their lack of manoeuvrability and the fact that spare parts were becoming increasingly hard to find (Reading was one of the last half dozen towns to run a trolley bus network) all told against them. The Rhodesian crisis, which pushed up the price of copper, also made an electric transport system more expensive.

And so the big six-wheelers trundled on their last journey, from the town centre to Tilehurst and back, photographed by hundreds of Reading people and by trolley bus fans from far and wide. The remaining vehicles in the fleet were either sold to other towns with trolley buses, to keep their services going; or were bought by enthusiasts, to drive their wives to distraction, or scrapped. In the following weeks the network of poles and wires also disappeared from the town's streets.

But the Reading public were not happy with their modernised public transport. The new one-man buses, which by now made up 70 per cent of the fleet, were described as 'cattle trucks' in a lively correspondence in the *Chronicle*. For its part the bus company was at pains to point out that the savings provided by one-man operation gave their ungrateful passengers possibly the lowest fares in the country.

As the trolley buses disappeared, so the heyday of the private car was symbolised by the opening of the Chatham Street multi-storey car park. With 1,000 spaces and a cost of £875,000, it was one of the biggest of its kind in the country at the time and was considered sufficiently advanced to attract the Minister of Transport, Richard Marsh, to come and open it. For the first week the public were allowed to use it for free, while they got the hang of multi-storey car parking. Thereafter, they were charged the grand sum of 1s for two hours, rising to 3s for 12 hours. A total of 350 spaces were reserved for contract parking, at a cost of £3 a month (a sum which would buy you just a few hours' parking today). Most users were full of praise for the new car park, though some still declared it to be too small, too expensive or too far from the town centre.

The new one-man buses, which by now made up 70 per cent of the fleet, were described as 'cattle trucks'

COUNTY BOROUGH OF READING

NEW CAR PARK

The Chatham Street Multi Storey Car Park
with accommodation for 1,000 Cars

OPEN

FROM MONDAY, 30th SEPTEMBER, 1968

FREE PARKING

UNTIL SATURDAY, 5th OCTOBER, 1968

SCALE OF CHARGES :

FIRST 2 hours	1s. 0d.	4 – 6 hours	2s. 6d.
2 – 3 hours	1s. 6d.	6 – 12 hours	3s. 0d.
3 – 4 hours	2s. 0d.	12 – 24 hours	4s. 0d.

OVERNIGHT PARKING (6 p.m. – 8 a.m.) 1s. 6d.
CONTRACT PARKING £3 0s 0d. per month

Built by J. M. JONES & SONS, LTD., OF MAIDENHEAD

1968 – Free parking, while Reading residents get the hang of the multi-storey car park.

In his opening speech, Richard Marsh acknowledged the pioneering role Reading had played in the transport field. The town had carried out a land use/transport study even before the best known pathfinder in this field, Colin Buchanan, had demonstrated the link between the two. Reading had also been one of the national leaders in developing bus lanes. Perhaps most significantly for the beleaguered residents of Pell Street and other town centre through routes, Marsh promised that the M4 would be finished by the end of 1971.

. . . BUT NO JAM TOMORROW

The economy of Reading was changing. The 1970s would see the town's three main traditional industries moving away, but one of the first major manufacturers to go was the Co-operative Jam Factory on Berkeley Avenue – the site of the famous pre-war fire. It announced its closure after ninety years in the town and at a cost of 189 jobs.

ROCK AND ROLL – HERE TO STAY?

1971

Britain votes to join Europe and the Angry Brigade bomb Government buildings. More fear and loathing as Reading hosts its first rock festival. Yet further hysteria at the launch of the Broad Street Mall. The M4 opens, giving many Reading residents their first good night's sleep in years.

Reading Rock Festival has been part of the town's life for at least a quarter of the twentieth century and has made the town's name internationally known, at least to 'layabouts, anarchists, drug-pushers, sexual perverts and other trouble makers' (not my words – I will return to them later). It started life as a jazz festival in Richmond in 1961 and later paid a brief visit to Windsor. In 1971 the Borough Council agreed to the principle of holding a pop festival in the town. It would be overstating the case to say that the idea was welcomed with rapturous enthusiasm by everybody. This was the *Chronicle*'s editorial on hearing the news:

Pop Festival Foreboding
Is it too late now for the Corporation to consider the desirability of rescinding permission for a pop festival to be held on land adjoining Richfield Avenue in late June as an adjunct to the Festival of Reading? Are they satisfied that the conditions they have so far laid down are adequate for the occasion?

The principal factor which gives rise to apprehension is the lack of control over numbers. It is not possible to forecast with any degree of certainty how many are likely to turn up for such an event, but given fine weather, pop groups and intensive advertising, the numbers could become overwhelming. It would not be easy, of course, to impose an enforceable limit, but unless the organisations give an undertaking that every means will be adopted to keep attendance to a figure which the authorities, and the Police in particular, consider reasonable, the Corporation should seriously reconsider the prudence of allowing such an event to go ahead.

If the local paper was unenthusiastic, some of the local residents went ballistic. This is just part of a letter which appeared in the following week's paper:

I read with much interest your comments in the 'opinion' column of the *Reading Chronicle* dated May 7. As the parent of teenage girls I am in fact extremely worried and most concerned for other local children, who are going to be exposed to considerable danger, both moral and otherwise.

I wonder how many parents really realise what this three-day festival is all about and have they forgotten the Isle of Wight Festival? The residents of that island certainly have not, even now much of the damage is still evident.

I question the intelligence of our Corporation which I would assume is run by responsible persons who have the welfare of the town and its citizens at heart. . . . I must say to the Mayor, Aldermen and Councillors, Why? Why? did you sanction such an event which, as past functions of this kind have shown, will attract some 50,000 or more young persons to this town, 10 per cent of whom will be layabouts, anarchists, drug-pushers, sexual perverts and other trouble-makers, who will only have come here to create havoc and corrupt our own young

'Have they forgotten the Isle of Wight Festival?'

1971 – And a multi-storey car park becomes the smart place to dine out in Reading.

children, because, let's face it, they will, despite even the strictest parental control. Many homes will have domestic upheavals; it is hard enough now when parents say No, you cannot go here or you cannot do that.

The site on which this event is scheduled to take place is in itself most unsuitable. From the point of view of control it is wide open, there are no suitable toilet facilities (unless the river is envisaged as an open sewer), there is no water supply, no suitable sleeping accommodation. . . .

I suggest that our Council think again and think very hard indeed before it is too late to retract the permission they have granted for our town to be defiled without even considering the wishes of the electorate whom they say they serve. They may find to their cost that this was a very unwise decision. Elections come and go, so can councillors, and the electorate are very sensitive, especially when it is likely to affect their own personal well-being and pockets.

Reading was about to be twinned with both Sodom and Gomorrah, it seemed – one Councillor even used that analogy. Others sought to rally protests from such diverse sources as the local MP, the Townswomen's Guild, the Women's Institute and Caversham Residents' Association. The promoters, for their part, were most put out at being pre-judged in this way. They replied that they were not associated with the Isle of Wight or any of the other festivals people complained about. Their track record was, they said, exemplary and all they wanted was a fair chance to prove themselves. They also claimed that the forecast attendance of 45,000 was ridiculous. If it were true, they would all be preparing to go to the Bahamas. None the less, companies with premises in the vicinity of the festival site flooded Securicor with requests for their services over the festival weekend.

There were even protests from a group you might have expected to be the festival's strongest supporters – Reading's rock and roll community. They complained that local bands had been excluded from the festival: 'No local band or agent heard so much as a whisper from the organising authorities and now it is too late to squeeze them into the programme. . . . there were a number of groups who would have been prepared to stand in as programme fillers, but they just have not had the chance.'

But as the organisers wearily pointed out: 'It is not our job to ring round small local groups. They should have come to us. If they had, we would have given them due consideration.'

Whilst responding to all these complaints, the promoters took the opportunity to announce the line-up of attractions for the festival. They described it as 'a selection of artists from just below the charts'. It was, the *Chronicle* said, 'impressive enough to attract thousands of pop fans from throughout the county and southern England. The programme includes one of the most comprehensive lists of heavy progressive groups ever assembled together and there are also sufficient folk artists to attract folk fans en masse.'

The final list of artists read as follows, and gives us a reminder (if one is required) of the transient nature of popular music fame. How many of these can you remember?

Friday: Arthur Brown, Warm Dust, Daddy Longlegs, Anno Domini, Clouds, Universe.

Saturday: Sha Na Na, Lindisfarne, Ralph McTell, Wishbone Ash, Stud, Gillian McPherson.

Sunday: Colosseum, Medicine Head, Van de Graaff Generator, Osibisa, Storyteller, Rory Gallagher and Demick and Armstrong.

The admission prices for this galaxy of talent were £2 for an all-weekend ticket (bought in advance) or, at the gate 50p for Friday and £1.50 for each of the other two days.

There was heavy rain as preparations for the festival went ahead. Some parts of the site were knee-deep in mud and water and had to be fenced off to prevent fans sinking to their doom. The only enclosure of the site as a whole was a 3-foot-high fence and the organisers posted 200 guards around the perimeter to keep trespassers out.

The police announced their own arrangements for the festival, and here at least there were no half measures. There were to be a total of 550 officers on hand, many of them imported from Buckinghamshire and Oxfordshire, with both aerial and river patrols to back them up. The cost of policing would be £17,000, part of which would be borne by the Borough Council. They anticipated making some fifty arrests a day, though no details were issued of any productivity bonus for their officers.

The fans began to arrive. Some of them came without money, hoping to get work on the festival site in return for free admission. With them came more rain and cold winds. Carters camping store did a roaring trade in polythene sheets at 60p a time, though they also reported a corresponding increase in shoplifting. Then the music started and the fans danced in the ever-deepening pools of mud. The crowds were variously estimated at between 20,000 and 50,000, depending on what point the person making the estimate wanted to prove.

One group of local people, at least, were converted to the idea of a pop festival:

Carters camping store did a roaring trade in polythene sheets at 60p a time, though they also reported a corresponding increase in shoplifting

Pop Festival Boost for Caversham Traders
After a weekend of thriving business, Caversham traders would back the suggestion to have another Festival next year. The fans, however, are not keen to return. Many left bitter about the organisation of the event with complaints about high prices on the site, the lack of good food, shelter and drinking water and a poor sound system. . . .

£35 p.w. by age 18

Join the Prudential and become an expert-we'll show you how.

If you like the idea, we'll be happy to train you to be one of our tip top Punch Card Operators feeding vital information into our computers. What's more we'll foot the expense—and pay you a full salary!

At the end of your training you will, with experience and application, be all set to push up your monthly earnings to the equivalent of £30, £35 or even £40 p.w. or more! It all depends upon your speed and efficiency—age isn't important to us. Salary revisions are frequent and you could earn four rises in a year.

If you have previous keyboard experience this will be taken into account when assessing your starting salary. We think you'll enjoy life at the Prudential. As well as a good salary, we provide a pleasant, light and spacious office, a staff restaurant and plenty of other fringe benefits. And you will be working with a young friendly crowd—just like you.

Get in touch with Mrs. Christine Braine now by completing and sending her this coupon. The address is: Staff Dept., Prudential Assurance Co. Ltd., Forbury House, 18-20 The Forbury, Reading RG1 3ES. Or you can telephone her on Reading 583511 ext. 243.

Please tell me all about being a Punch Card Operator at the Prudential.

Name_____

Address_____

BIP_____Age_____

Prudential

Reading workers learn new-fangled computer skills in the 1970s.

Several fans complained that it was the most uncomfortable and disorganised pop event they had ever been to and one of them, John May from London, said 'The ground was waterlogged and the police were breathing down our necks'.

Local businesses, however, loved the event:

Mrs S. Parsons who, with her husband, manages a confectionery shop, said 'The fans were absolutely marvellous, despite their appearance. We took a lot of money.'

The proprietor of an establishment known as the Bake 'n' Take agreed:

I found the pop fans wonderful, nice, polite people. There was not a single incident all weekend. I stayed open until 1 and 2 a.m. on Friday and Saturday and did marvellous trade.

Also doing marvellous trade were the police. They searched over a thousand of those entering the site and were roundly condemned by the fans for their over-zealous policing. Some 144 fans found themselves appearing before a specially convened court that was working overtime throughout the weekend. An organisation called ADE was set up by Reading University students to assist those attending the festival and it became an unofficial spokesman for the fans. Among the various statements and newsletters issued by ADE in the course of the weekend were many pieces of hippy wisdom:

This is Reading's first Pop Festival and the straights are in a panic. The Thames Valley Drugs Squad have a heavy reputation for busts and they aim to keep it. So be cool about smoking and don't buy any dope on the site.

The Marquee Organisation, despite their ultimate good intentions, are badly organised to deal with the real needs of the people. The Festival site is at present a mess. Last night, hundreds of people had to sleep on a cold rainy night with only polythene to cover them.

This Festival is a very heavy trip and we all know why. The ultimate responsibility must lie with the Reading Borough Council who leased the ground to the Marquee Organisation. They know full well the kind of people the Festival would be catering for; people like you of the drug sub-culture. But having got the thing together, they arranged or allowed the Thames Valley Police to act out their fantasies of a police state by busting or hassling as many longhairs as they could get hold of.

Despite ADE's exhortations to be cool about using drugs, several of the policemen disguised as hippies (presumably the ones with flowers in their helmets) found unwitting drug-dealers offering them exotic substances. But not all of these narcotics were as exotic as they were made out to be. Oxo cubes were being offered as cannabis resin (giving rise to the expression 'stocked out of your mind'. Surely the silver paper around them gave them away?); dyed aspirins were offered as LSD (not much of a trip, but no headache afterwards); and one dealer certainly could not be charged under the Trades Descriptions Act when he asked: 'Want to buy some grass, man?' For what he was selling was precisely that – very expensive dried grass. At one of the subsequent year's festivals, someone was even trying to pass off pasta shapes as LSD tablets – before being arrested for carrying macaroni with a street value of £23,000.

Perhaps the unluckiest fan in this regard was the youth at a subsequent year's festival, who paid £10 for some drugs, only to find that he had been sold caffeine tablets. Though not normally a dealer himself, he decided to try to recoup his losses by selling them on. He looked around for the most gormless and gullible-looking rock fans he could see, and offered them the goods. The two drugs squad detectives he approached accepted his offer gratefully and took him into custody, where the caffeine tablets cost him a further £130 in fines for going equipped to cheat.

A 'bust fund' was set up by ADE to assist those who had come to the attention of the police and by Monday morning it had raised £400. As the fund-raisers so elegantly put it: 'If we can get enough money to pay all the fines, then the fuzz have just wasted their time and the taxpayers' money. Love to you all. Off the pigs.' In fact, they fell some way short of paying all the fines. By the end of the festival, magistrates had imposed a total of £1,737 in fines and £260 in costs. At least the police were not distracted from their pursuit of Oxo salesmen by much in the way of

arrested for carrying macaroni with a street value of £23,000 physical violence. There were threats of confrontations between Hell's Angels and skinheads at the Festival, but these did not materialise.

One body which was represented at the festival was the Church. The Bishop of Portsmouth set up a Christian tent on the site, and it even attracted about 150 people to a Sunday morning service. The local vicar who manned the tent over the weekend described it as 'quite an education'.

So the first Reading Pop Festival came to an end amid controversy and recrimination. Many fans got to the station too late to catch their trains, and spent the night sleeping on the platforms. Few at the time would have put much money on the festival becoming the institution that it subsequently has.

Those who feared that the festival would bring the excesses of the permissive society to Reading were wrong. It was already here, on sale in a newsagents in Southampton Street. The proprietor appeared in court, charged with selling over 150 obscene books and magazines, along with an assortment of indecent photos. The magistrates clearly felt that permissiveness was passing them by:

Earlier, the Chairman had asked if he and his fellow Magistrates could see some of the literature, as they had not had the opportunity of seeing how obscene or depraved it was.

Mr Blackburn Gittings, defending, advised 'I have seen these magazines, and it is difficult to imagine anything more obscene'.

Not, you may think, the most helpful interjection for the defence counsel to make on behalf of his client, but at least the magistrates decided in the light of it to rely upon the infinite resources of their imagination. They fined the defendant £200, plus £20 costs, without having sampled the goods.

It was a time of great change for Reading, and the town's long-serving Chief Executive, Harry Tee, shared his thoughts on the town's future with the readers of the *Chronicle*:

The nearly completed M4 will remove some through traffic from the town, but it will cause only a slight reduction in the volume of traffic in the central area; a cut which may well be entirely offset by the growth in the use of cars over the next few years.

This traffic congestion delays, deters and even prevents people reaching the centre. In peak hours it can only be solved by new attitudes to mass transport, leading to a quick and convenient journey between home and work. The commuter should be prepared to expect severe restrictions on the use of their transport to achieve this end but I wonder how long, if ever, it will be before such a change of heart takes place?

. . . In a few years, high speed trains will mean that Paddington will be within only a few minutes' journey of the Reading central station. Will a shorter service entice commuters to travel in the reverse direction to occupy the office blocks which land speculators are waiting to build in Reading, or would it be better if some of these pleasant sites close to the Thames Meadows, the Kennet and the town centre were used for high density housing?

. . . Traffic not destined for the town centre must be channelled around the edges, making the central area a more peaceful and comfortable place to shop in. It is for this purpose that the Inner Distribution Road is being constructed. When this has been completed, active steps can be taken to extend the Broad Street

Early attempts to manage the growing traffic outside Reading station, just before the outbreak of war. They thought they had problems . . .

pedestrianisation experiment into other areas of the town centre, such as the Market Place.

. . . The new commercial centre will be a demonstration of what can be achieved by co-operation between the Corporation and a progressive development company. I hope it will be the forerunner of a new era of enlightened developments in the town.

The new commercial centre to which he refers is that jewel of Reading's architecture known to us today as the Broad Street Mall. As for the pedestrianisation of Broad Street of which he speaks, this was not the traffic-free environment we know today. Even once it was free from the all-purpose traffic which had made crossing the road a lottery, Broad Street was still used as the town's major bus interchange, and the pedestrians were in almost as much danger from public transport as they were from the private car. Once it opened, Broad Street Mall (or, as it was then known, the Butts Centre) was almost overwhelmed by its own success. A lighting shop called Lampshades persuaded Coronation Street stars Len Fairclough and Elsie Tanner to perform the opening ceremony. They drew a crowd of about 4,000 and, in the mêlée to get to see them, the mob did some £1,000 worth of damage to the shop, with smashed plate glass windows and broken chandeliers.

READING TO LOSE ITS INDEPENDENCE

Another major change for the town would be the restructuring of local government. The outcome of this would be that Reading, after its long history of independent local government, ended up sharing its powers with Berkshire County Council. The changes would not take place until 1974, but there was already lively discussion about the emerging proposals in 1971. Berkshire County Council itself faced a radical boundary review, with large parts of its western end – areas such as Abingdon, Faringdon, Wallingford and Wantage – going off into Oxfordshire. In return the county was due to get Slough and (over the dead bodies of many of its residents) Henley. Some county councillors questioned whether giving up an Area of Outstanding Natural Beauty in return for Slough was a fair swap. They were told that Slough came complete with Eton as a consolation prize, but they remained unconvinced. The new county, one said, would have about as much identity as Middlesex and would be submerged by the urban areas of Slough and Reading.

Another complained in this debate that the decision about the County Council would affect the residents of Berkshire for the next hundred years. This proved not to be the case. Less than a quarter of a century later, in 1998, Berkshire County Council itself disappeared and Reading returned to the self-contained local government that it had enjoyed for most of the town's long history. Henley meanwhile successfully resisted all attempts to push it into Berkshire.

SILENT NIGHT: THE M4 OPENS FOR CHRISTMAS

The last big event of 1971 was the opening of the M4 motorway just before Christmas. The need for the road was first identified, by both central and local government, as long ago as the 1930s and no fewer than seven alternative routes were considered in the 1950s and 1960s. One of them – admitted later to be an administrative error – had the road ploughing through the middle of Chieveley. One side-effect of the motorway's construction was the need for something like six million cubic yards of gravel, most of which was extracted from 370 acres of land between Theale and Holyport. Much of this land was later returned to cultivation, but one lasting souvenir of the building of the M4 is the lake at Dinton Pastures.

The opening ceremony was performed by one Michael Heseltine, then a mere Under-Secretary of State at the Environment Department. He had had the chance to drive down the motorway the day before the opening. At the opening, which took place in pouring rain at Holyport, he made much of the fact that it was now possible to travel from London to Bristol in two hours (forgetting that the railway had been doing it in rather less than that for years). The Bishop of Oxford was also on hand to bless the road. Then, in a triumph for British engineering, the ministerial Jaguar refused to start and, having established that it was beyond even the Bishop's powers of prayer, the police had to push it away. Mr Heseltine boarded one of a fleet of coaches and set off for Chippenham, and further opening celebrations.

Early travel on the motorway was not without incident. At one point motorists found themselves swerving to avoid hounds and hunt servants from the Duke of Beaufort's Hunt, which were milling around on the motorway after a fox very inconsiderately ran the wrong way. Mud and stones left on the carriageway by the contractors caused dozens of smashed windscreens and the fact that there were at first no motorway services between west London and the Severn bridge left motorists at serious risk of running out of petrol. The lack of motorway services brought an unexpected bonus for businesses near the motorway. The petrol filling station at Three Mile Cross found itself doing two or three times its normal business and the Tower Cafe at Theale reported no drop-off in business, despite traffic switching from the A4 to the M4.

In a triumph for British engineering, the ministerial Jaguar refused to start

The impact of the road on Reading was even more dramatic. A 25 per cent reduction in east–west traffic through the town had been forecast, but surveys showed it was actually down by 60 per cent, with the possibility of further reductions once the Christmas rush was out of the way. Ironically, though, north–south traffic got much worse, as people from Caversham and South Oxfordshire made their way to and from the M4. Queues built up at Caversham and Reading Bridges, Caversham Road suffered serious congestion and Whitley Councillor Ken Darvall described the M4 as 'a calamity' for his ward, as the Basingstoke Road snarled up.

But in the town centre many people living along the A4 got their first decent night's sleep for years, untroubled by the noise of heavy lorries. They could even sleep with the windows open, leaving aside for a moment the fact that it was December. Some even complained that they found the silence hard to get used to. Meanwhile, others to the south of the town, living near the motorway, had to get used to the idea of 4,000 vehicles an hour going past them – in some cases, within 30 feet of their back doors.

BULBS – SUTTONS GO WEST

1974

Industrial strife and the three-day week begin the year – the Conservative Government is brought down. Suttons end a 160-year link with the town. Caversham Park residents denounce Reading as entertainment 'dragsville' and a start is made on the Hexagon.

Suttons Seeds were one of the three great employers in nineteenth-century Reading. At the height of their importance, their town centre premises occupied much of the area on the east side of Market Place, between the Forbury, Abbey Street and Kings Road, and their trial grounds were a feature of the eastern approaches to the town. The firm had its origins in a seed and corn merchants, founded in 1807 by John Sutton. But it was the business acumen of his son, Martin Hope Sutton, that set them on the road to large-scale success. He began trading on his own account in 1828, when he was just thirteen, and quickly gained a reputation for reliability in an industry which was not noted for it at the time. The family took an active part in the public life of the town, providing some of its mayors and helping to found the college which eventually became Reading University.

It seemed as if Suttons' long association with Reading would continue indefinitely. In 1961 they announced plans to erect a large new building on 4 acres of their London Road trial grounds. It would give them, they said, the most modern seed establishment in the country. They also gave assurances that they would keep their Market Place shop open. But the ties began to loosen. In 1966 their long association with Market Place ended. Shortly after a merger with Edward Webb and Co., Suttons closed their town centre premises and concentrated their activities on their London Road site. The real shock was to come in February 1974:

Men's outfitting from 1974 – the decade that fashion forgot.

Suttons decide to quit town shock. Move to Torquay being planned

Suttons Seeds Managing Director Mr Frank Hunt dropped a bombshell yesterday when he revealed that the company intend to move their entire business to the west country.

The announcement that the company will move follows similar moves recently announced by Huntley & Palmers and Courage's, the other two traditional industries in the town. It means that the 'three Bs' – beer, biscuits and bulbs – which made Reading famous, could disappear from the town.

The firm, who have for so many years led the way in the flower and vegetable garden world, may now desert their home town for the more favourable seed-growing climate of the south west.

One of the reasons they gave for their departure was that the roundabout at the end of the A329(M) motorway link had taken part of their trial ground, and that future extensions of that road (now the link road into the Thames Valley Business Park) would affect more of it. But there were more immediate reasons than that for their move. Suttons had for some years had difficulty recruiting casual labour in Reading for their main packing season, which extended through the winter months. By moving to Torquay, their seasonal labour requirements tied in perfectly with the town's other big industry, tourism.

About 600 workers in Reading would be affected, though those who were prepared to uproot and move with the firm to Torquay were promised jobs at the other end. Suttons may not have been expecting too many of their staff to make that move, since they had also promised the planning authorities in Devon that their relocation would create 145 new full-time and up to 320 part-time jobs for the residents of Torquay.

There was one other small consideration that may have prompted their move. It was the fact that they were sitting on a goldmine. Just a week after their move was made public, Suttons announced – in apparent surprise – that they had been inundated with offers for their London Road site. Property agents estimated that the site was worth around £90,000 an acre for industrial development, giving Suttons a leaving present worth well over £5 million.

The A329(M) was just being opened as Suttons announced their departure. Whatever impact the roundabout had on Sutton's trial grounds, the improved motorway access that it gave to their site did no harm whatsoever to the industrial value of their remaining land. It was described at the time as a 'costly and controversial' road. Campaigners living along its line were opposed to the road from the start, though it was quite clear that the existing Wokingham Road could not have coped with the extra traffic the M4 motorway would create between it and the centre of Reading. The need to put part of the new route in a cutting, and to build an 1100-foot-long viaduct over the Loddon Valley, helped to push the cost of the 2½ mile road up to £5.5 million. The construction itself had been marred by tragedy, when in October 1972 a section of the road at Loddon Bridge collapsed, killing three construction workers. Current users of the road might care to note that it was designed to carry 25,000 vehicles a day. At the last count, it was taking rather more than double that number.

VILLAGE GOSSIP

By 1974 Caversham Park Village was firmly part of the built-up area of Reading (though, administratively, it would remain within South Oxfordshire until 1977). Some 1,500 houses had been built on 180 acres of the former Caversham Park Estate and the developers at least spoke very highly of it. They had:

Caversham Park House, seen from the air, with part of Caversham Park village under construction, c. 1970.

planned the estate as a pleasant residential area where families can live without constant noise and traffic. . . . The principle behind the vehicle and pedestrian separation is known as the Radburn system and it has already proved effective in America and Scandinavia. This was the first private sector development of any size in this country to feature the Radburn system and much imagination went into the planning and creation of the village.

So, it was not that the houses were all built back to front – they were meant to be that way!

A survey of Caversham Park Village was carried out at the time by seventy-five volunteers, with the aim of penetrating the innermost soul of the average resident. It revealed that he – or she – had arrived on the estate in 1969, was married with 1.2 children, went swimming in his – or her – spare time and would like to play badminton or squash if the facilities were available. The Village was evidently a whirl of social activity, with four football teams, a netball team for the ladies, a food group with so many members that they did not have anywhere large enough to meet, and clubs for everything from stamp collecting and bridge through to water sports and rifle shooting. All of the Village's activities (or at least those fit to print) were recorded in the estate's own newspaper, *Village Voice*.

The Village was evidently a whirl of social activity

This journal had earned itself a moment of notoriety in 1968 with an editorial denouncing Reading as 'Dragsville'. This suggested that, apart from its leading department store and, possibly, its library, Reading had nothing to commend it. The residents of the Village should, in the contributor Bumpkin's view, look elsewhere for its amenities or provide them for itself. This attracted howls of rage from deliriously happy residents who found Reading to be entertainment heaven, and forced an apology from the Caversham Park Village Association.

The development of the estate had a long history. The land was first earmarked for housing in a plan drawn up in 1954, for completion by about 1974. It was originally envisaged as overspill Council housing for Reading but, for whatever reason, Reading Borough Council had not made any progress in developing it by 1959. In that year a change in the law took away the preferential terms on which local authorities could compulsorily purchase land for housing and it was effectively priced out of the Council's reach. The land increased in value by more than tenfold overnight.

The new purchasers, Davis Contractors, had to go to appeal to get planning permission for their development in 1961. The few local residents of the day, represented by the Eye and Dunsden Parish Council, objected to the very principle of development, 'because it is a pleasant stretch of parkland, enjoying very pleasant views over the Thames Valley and could have become a local beauty spot.' However, if development must take place, the Parish preferred it to be owner-occupied, since owner-occupation was a good thing in itself; it would be more in keeping with the area; and because private development would generate a higher rateable value and thus not be a burden on the local taxpayer.

READING GETS ITS VERSAILLES
In the town centre the go-ahead was finally given for the next part of the Civic Centre complex – a new, purpose-built concert hall and

entertainments centre. It was due to be completed in 1976/77, at a cost of £1.74 million, though its name – The Hexagon – was not yet announced. The cost went steadily up throughout the construction period so that by the time it opened in October 1977 it was referred to as Reading's £4 million concert hall – or roughly £2,400 per seat. But the centre's new manager promised the people of Reading that their investment would be rewarded with a varied diet of wrestling, brass band concerts, fashion shows and debates.

Throughout the building period, its critics could complain about the escalating construction costs. Once it was open, they also had the running costs to moan about. By 1980 it was alleged to cost £1.25 million a year to keep it open, despite it attracting 250,000 visits that year. The Reading Ratepayers' Association condemned it as a latterday Versailles, and called for it to break even or to be closed.

BISCUITS – HUNTLEY & PALMER STOP BAKING

1977

The nation celebrates the Queen's Silver Jubilee. Huntley & Palmer produce their last biscuits in Reading. Punk rock and soccer hooliganism come to the town.

More than any other Reading company, Huntley & Palmer spread the town's name to the farthest corners of the earth. Reading was home to the world's largest biscuit factory, whose products were to be found up the most remote mountains and in the depths of jungles impenetrable to all but biscuit salesmen. At the outbreak of the First World War, six thousand people worked in their factories on either side of the Kennet & Avon Canal in Reading.

The company was founded by Joseph Huntley at 72 London Street, serving coach passengers stopping at the nearby Crown Inn. One of the secrets of the company's success was its link with their neighbours, the London Street ironmongers Huntley, Boorne & Stevens, who made tinplate boxes to keep the biscuits fresh and unbroken during their travels.

The Palmer family, in particular, were very active in the life of the town and were great benefactors to it. They acquired part of King's Meadow for the town, built model housing estates for their workforce and helped fund the town's museum and the emerging university. They also provided the park in east Reading which bears the family name.

During the Second World War, Huntley & Palmer's biscuits were 'zoned' – that is, their sales were banned in the more distant parts of the country, in order to save transport costs. In 1955 labour shortages in Reading, coupled with a desire to strengthen their representation in the north of the country, led the company to build a state-of-the-art automated factory at Huyton, near Liverpool, and then, almost immediately, to extend it. Some assumed that similar automation would come to the Reading factory but in the early 1970s it was announced that

Reading was home to the world's largest biscuit factory, whose products were to be found up the most remote mountains and in the depths of jungles impenetrable to all but biscuit salesmen

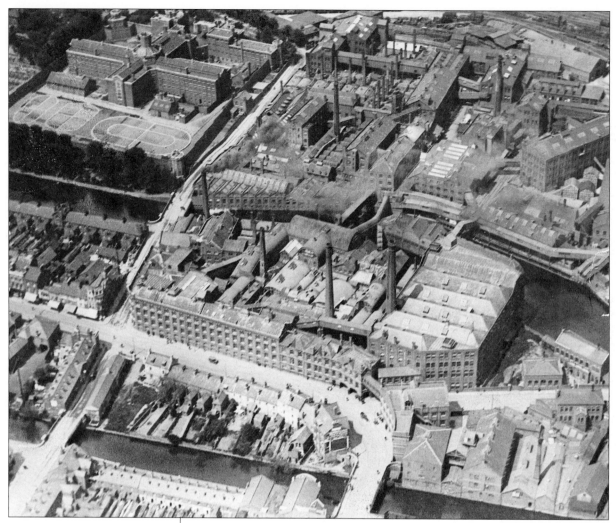

Huntley & Palmer's factories from the south-west, 1925.

biscuit manufacture would end altogether in Reading. By 1977 Reading had baked its last Huntley & Palmer biscuit. However, the old factory buildings were still used for storage of biscuits made elsewhere and in February 1980 a fire in a semi-demolished part of the premises almost cost them £100,000 worth of stock, which was being stored in the next building. The fire closed the Forbury Road as firemen fought to prevent 750 tonnes of teatime assorted going up in smoke.

Reading's association with biscuit-making was not entirely finished. In 1982 Nabisco bought Huntley & Palmer Foods (which included other household names of the biscuit variety such as Jacobs and Peek Frean) and by 1989 their entire biscuit operation had been renamed 'The Jacob's Bakery Ltd'. In 1991, the 150th anniversary of Mr Huntley joining Mr Palmer in their historic partnership, Jacobs opened their group's new head office on the Sutton's Business Park – the former site of Sutton's bulb-testing grounds.

PALAIS DE POLICE
As one industry was lost, so another was expanding. Princess Anne came to Reading in February 1977 to open the new £2.5 million police headquarters

'Allo, 'allo, what's all this here? Princess Anne opens the new police station, 1977.

in Castle Street. There was a dispute about the £3,481 of this sum which was spent on pot plants (presumably not the kind confiscated at the pop festival) to brighten up the building. Stung by this criticism, the police became so cost-conscious that they did not even provide their royal guest with a plaque to unveil. She had to sign the visitors' book instead – one of the few visitors to do so without having to turn out their pockets first.

The police were not short of work on Saturday afternoons, for this was a time when football hooliganism was a constant problem. Few home games at Elm Park seemed to pass without some report of disturbances. One of the worst of these came in March 1977, when a group of Portsmouth supporters very nearly kicked a Reading fan to death. In a day dubbed 'Bloody Saturday' by the press, a total of sixty-two arrests (fifty-six of them Portsmouth fans) were made. Windows of shops, houses and cars near the ground were smashed and there were running battles with the police both before and after the match. Four of the fans who carried out the kicking were traced and were sentenced to up to four years for grievous bodily harm. In another, so-called 'friendly', match against Charlton just a few weeks afterwards, police were assaulted and a youth was stabbed.

UNDERGROUND READING
Up in Emmer Green there were problems linked to some new flats being built at the junction of Peppard Road and Kiln Road. During the course of

*Punk band 'The Jam' play at
Reading's Top Rank Suite, 1977.*

construction, a vast 200-year-old chalk mine was discovered some 50 feet below the site. It was large enough to take two double-decker buses and an estimated 100 yards long, stretching across Peppard Road and under some houses on the far side. Dates – some as early as 1777 – were found scratched on its walls and relics left behind by the miners, such as clay pipes and old shoes, were also recovered. It was thought to be seventy or eighty years since the mine had been last worked. The chalk was apparently mined to line the kilns of the nearby brickworks and also to whiten bread in the days before more sophisticated chemicals were available to bakers. A survey of the mine was quickly commissioned and it established – much to everybody's relief – that the mine posed no threat to any of the housing in the area.

More threatening – to some people's minds – was another underground phenomenon that appeared in Reading in June 1977:

A naughticultural night out.
Studded collars, torn T-shirts as punk rock hits Reading.
Punk rock hit Reading this week. The latest 'sound' which produced the notorious Sex Pistols and an insulting version of 'God Save the Queen' attracted hundreds of youngsters to Reading's Top Rank suite on Monday. They wore torn T-shirts, razor blade earrings, nose rings and studded dog collars. The music that was to stir up the hysteria was wild, frenetic and, above all, loud. The group, the Jam, consisted of three boys; their cropped hair, Beatle-style suits and winklepicker shoes in stark contrast to the style of the fans.

Although the scene is comparable to the rock and roll concerts of the 1960s, the violence in the air was unique. The brand of music, called 'New Wave' by the fans, produced the tense atmosphere that has earned it the stigma of 'punk rock' in London.

Some 500 fans paid £1 each to see the band play a set of less than an hour. One eighteen-year-old fan, elegantly attired in a schoolboy's white shirt, black tights, dark glasses and with a hangman's noose around her waist, explained its attraction: 'The words don't matter. What is important is that you can do anything to the music. Nobody cares here.'

What most of the fans did with their new-found freedom was apparently to bounce up and down wildly, flailing their arms about, with a look on their faces that managed to be simultaneously hostile and vacant.

Local entrepreneur John Kennedy set the residents of Caversham frothing with indignation at the news that he was planning to buy the Glendale Cinema as a seven-

Punk fans – dressed to shock – enjoy a night out in Reading, 1977.

days-a-week punk rock club. He had previously aroused local anger by trying to stage a huge punk rock concert somewhere in the Reading area. The Glendale was closing after sixty-six years, in the face of rising losses. But Mr Kennedy had competition for the property. A group of old film lovers (lovers of old films, that is) had set up a fighting fund to save it and had soon amassed the grand sum of £100. The idea was to run a cinema that concentrated on the harmless escapism produced by Hollywood between 1920 and 1950, free of sex and violence. Spokesman for the film-buffs, Mr Eric Lilley of Tilehurst, explained: 'It would cater for people who like these kind of films – family people. This is something we need, not just for Reading, but for the whole of the south of England.'

The owner of the cinema pointed out wearily that the campaigners had no conception of the economics of running such an enterprise, and sold the building to the New Testament Church of God for a reported sum of around £40,000. In the golden years of the cinema, the Glendale had had no difficulty in filling its 900 seats every night, but it was just one of a number of victims of the competition from television. The Granby on London Road closed within four months of the Glendale and other postwar losses included the Savoy on Basingstoke Road, the Rex in Tilehurst, the Regal in Caversham and the Vaudeville in Broad Street.

The growth of Reading had by now spread far beyond its local government boundaries. Plans were announced in 1977 for a new town of 18,000 people at Lower Earley, in the administrative area of Wokingham. It had been the subject of years of negotiation, since the idea was first mooted in 1969. One of its main themes was to be affordable housing, with prices starting at £13,000 or less. The developers saw a big demand for them:

There is a lot of industry moving into the Reading area and this new town will encourage them. The main concern for people moving into the area is the shortage of housing. We hope to solve this problem. Reading is an expanding place and is going to get larger over the next twenty years. It has a steady employment record, even in these days of economic restraint. We will soon be seeing the benefits of North Sea Oil, which will increase the standard of living.

This was also the year of Silver Jubilee fever, when celebrations of a kind not seen in Reading since the Coronation marked the Queen's twenty-five years on the throne. Courage brewed extra beer, local bakers had a run on sausage rolls, bunting was sold by the mile and Corona reported their soft drinks takings up by 100 per cent as the town celebrated. Among many other events, the Silver Jubilee was marked by street parties, an industries exhibition in Caversham Court, a Caribbean Carnival parade, crazy river races and a greasy pole contest.

1978

CIVIC PRIDE

The winter of discontent begins, bringing chaos throughout Britain. The Queen opens the new Civic Offices and the Magistrates' Courts. Reading wonders what to do with half a ring road.

*Social Security – a form of unemployment benefit paid to people not on the Civil List.

The royal family were surprisingly infrequent visitors to the county town of Royal Berkshire, considering that Windsor Castle makes them almost next-door-neighbours. The Queen came to Reading just three times in the thirty-two years up to 1978: to see a circus at Hills Meadow in 1946, to open the Faculty of Letters at the University in 1957, and to inspect the Social Security* computer centre on Queens Road in 1968.

The Queen and Prince Philip returned in 1978 to open what was then seen as the first part of an ambitious civic centre complex, incorporating the Civic Offices, the Hexagon, and the Magistrates' Courts. The Mayor of Reading, Councillor Bill Mander, met them outside the Butts Centre and escorted them past the waving crowds. They toured the Civic Offices, where assorted members of staff were assembled in simulated work-mode. They inspected models of local authority housing schemes and Prince Philip took particular interest in plans for the new brewery, then under construction at Worton Grange. He was also much taken by the clocking-in machines in the Civic Offices, suggesting to his hosts that the staff could clock in in the mornings and then retire to the nearest pub – the limitations of the licensing hours apparently not being a problem for royalty. He also asked the hapless staff whether there were any Scottish Nationalist members on the Council. (This is now widely believed to have been a Royal Joke.)

The Queen goes walkabout during the opening of the Civic Centre complex in 1978.

In the Hexagon, the royal party rose into the auditorium on the lift from under the stage, much like pantomime fairies, to greet the assembled throng. They also toured the Magistrates' Courts, where much amusement was derived from the sight of civic dignitaries occupying the dock, in order to get a better view.

The construction of the courts had had a troubled history. Two of the three builders involved in their construction went bankrupt, and there were disputes about which of them were responsible for the faults which had delayed its completion and opening.

The royals met many people on their visit, ranging from avid royalists, bearing banners saying 'Liz rules o.k.' (correct, if obvious) to the anti-monarchist Labour Councillor Bob Garnett, who exchanged pleasantries with her, but was not converted from his republican views by the occasion.

The last phase of the Civic Centre, originally conceived in 1959, involved ambitious plans to bridge over the access road to the Butts Centre car park and build a new cultural centre. The scheme never materialised. The 'temporary' fences separating this phase of the civic area from the rest were still in place at the time of writing this book (1998). The centre would have provided a new and enlarged museum and art gallery, a central library and space for community activities – or, as the architects put it: 'A centre for communication, both supplying information and providing a context for social involvement and interaction.' But the words 'Cultural Centre' were easier to fit on to the wall.

The Cultural Centre that never was. An artist's impression of the main entrance, looking along Hosier Street from St Mary's Butts.

It was an ingenious building, designed to lure the public into it. It even had pedestrian routes running through its centre. It would have completed the civic complex, tying it more firmly into the town centre. It was to have been funded from the sale – and proposed demolition – of Reading's Victorian Town Hall, but the outcry against the loss of this much-loved landmark forced the Council to work up a refurbishment option instead. The estimated cost of restoring it fluctuated wildly and, at one stage, a skating rink and a cinema were among seventeen different options for its re-use being considered by the Council.

The need for the Borough Council to move from the old Town Hall to more spacious accommodation was first identified in 1901. A host of sites were considered, including the Forbury Gardens, London Road, Reading Prison, Hills Meadow and Prospect Park, and two world wars also intervened to delay matters. Thus, as we have seen, it was a mere three-quarters of a century later that the new Civic Offices opened. At the time of writing this, the refurbishment of the old Town Hall looks set to be completed just in time for the millennium.

READING'S SKI-JUMP

The Council's mind was also focused at the time on how to deal with its traffic problems. Central to its plans for many years was an Inner Distribution Road, which would carry traffic around the town centre. This road was another scheme with a long history. It was first proposed in the 1953 Reading Development Plan, which gained Government approval in 1957. The plans were firmed up in 1964 and approved by two separate government ministers in 1966. In 1971 the section from Caversham Road to Southampton Street was opened. Then came the local government reorganisation of 1974, when Reading lost its transport planning powers and work on the road ground to a halt. For years the Southampton Street end finished in a prominent 'ski jump'.

The original scheme would have carried a road over Kings Road and Abbey Square and under the Forbury Gardens. The 1960s Prudential building, which stood opposite the Forbury Gardens until 1998, was even constructed with a hole in the middle to accommodate a road which was never built. By the latter part of the 1970s an alternative was being considered, swinging out wider around the town centre and using the alignment of existing roads – the so-called 'Queens Road Alternative'.

Many people on Reading Borough Council were opposed to it. Liberal leader Jim Day condemned it as a 'cheap and nasty' scheme, which failed to separate public transport from pedestrians. Whether, at a cost at the time of £10.9 millions (as against £13.7m for the original scheme), it can be described as particularly 'cheap', as well as 'nasty', is another matter. Labour Councillor Tony Page said: 'We will fight the County Council all the way through a public inquiry and we are confident that we will kill the scheme stone dead.' Unfortunately for them, the County Council for the time being held the whip hand as the highway authority, and it was this scheme which finally got built, opening in 1989.

Aerial view of the Inner Distribution Road, Caversham Road to Southampton Street – Bridge Street – Mill Lane roundabout, 1972.

1980

BEER – BRIDGE STREET BREWERY CLOSES

Mrs Thatcher says she's not for turning and gets a hostile reception at the Hexagon. Courage's Brewery moves out of Reading – just – and national unemployment passes two million for the first time since 1935.

Courage staff celebrate the last brew at the old brewery, 1980.

Simonds' Brewery was the last of the triumvirate of great Victorian employers to leave central Reading. It was also the oldest, being founded originally in premises on Broad Street by William Simonds in 1785. He set up the brewery in Bridge Street, which was to be the centre of the company's activity for nearly two hundred years, in 1790.

The Simonds' first family home was Seven Bridges House, which was built on the site of the brewery, and which survives on Bridge Street to this day. They later moved to Caversham Court, a riverside mansion next to St Peter's Church in Caversham. They demolished a Tudor house on the site and replaced it with a mansion built by the architect Pugin, the demolition of which by the Council is covered earlier in this book. The Simonds family also diversified into banking. The bank building on King's Street, occupied at the time of writing by Barclays Bank, was originally built for them. The Simonds' brass plate is still on display outside the door.

Simonds' Brewery was finally devoured by the Courage empire in 1960 and then became part of the Imperial Tobacco Group in 1972. In the following year plans were announced to redevelop their long-standing site in the town centre. For a time it seemed as if another of the three Bs would be lost to the town entirely, with the loss of a further 1,100 jobs in the town.

But in 1974, just as Suttons were announcing their plans to leave the town, the possibility was raised of moving the brewery to a new 70 acre site at Worton Grange, near Junction 11 of the M4 on the outskirts of Reading. At first this site was only one of a number of options, but it soon became the favoured one. When a planning application was made for the new brewery, the main objection came from the real ale campaigners CAMRA, on the grounds that the old brewery made proper beer, whereas the new £60 million brewery, one of the biggest in Europe, would – they claimed – manufacture 1.5 million barrels of fizz per year. 'To kill off real ale is to destroy a part of Reading's community life and amenities', they told the Council. Any real ale-loving councillors may have been sympathetic to their argument, but the Planning Acts were mysteriously silent on the subject of keg lager as grounds for a refusal of planning permission.

The last beer was brewed at the old Bridge Street premises in 1980. One of the problems with their new location was the illogical nature of the local government boundaries around Reading, which meant that the new brewery at Worton Grange was built half in Reading, and half in Wokingham, paying their local government taxes to both and complaining to – who knows where? – if services were not up to standard. A similar problem arose with regard to the University campus, where individual buildings were split in two by boundaries that had been drawn up many years before its current use was envisaged.

The Labour protest march passes the old Prudential building – the one with the hole for the Inner Distribution Road, 1980.

Crowd trouble at Reading v. Southampton in 1978. A fan helps police with their inquiries.

Reading Football Club was still suffering from the effects of the many hooligans turning up to its games. After an incident in which a fan ran on to the pitch and assaulted a player, there was a threat from the FA to close the stadium if steps were not taken to contain hooliganism. The club responded by erecting crowd barriers. They were in place just in time for a visit by Millwall and their notorious fans – the F Troop, led by Harry the Dog.

This was a visit that some people were to remember for a long time. Denied the opportunity of a decent punch-up at the ground itself, there were riots and pitched battles between police and fans all along the Oxford Road. About seventy of the hooligans invaded the Captain's Cabin in West Street, smashed the place up and put three people, including the landlady, into hospital. Eight people later appeared in court.

A nicer class of disorder took place at the Hexagon, where a large crowd of protesters gathered to lobby the new Prime Minister, Margaret Thatcher, as she arrived to address a conference of Conservative trade unionists. The police very unsportingly smuggled her in through a back entrance and the protesters, denied a target for their indignation, marched off to a meeting in Reading Town Hall. The Mayor, Councillor Absolom, added to the furore by deciding to stay at home with her family, rather than welcome what some described as Britain's first lady to the town. Others thought that the Queen still held that title.

Finally, long-standing Reading residents may remember the cast-iron Victorian urinals that stood beside Caversham Bridge for many years. A heated debate was under way in 1980 as to their future. One Councillor described them rather ambitiously as 'having more architectural merit than the Town Hall' and various imaginative options – such as conversion into an information centre or a tea room – were being canvassed. Eventually, they found their way to an open air museum, where they could continue in their intended function.

THE GREAT STORM

1987

The ferry Herald of Free Enterprise *capsizes outside Zeebrugge Harbour; hundreds of passengers are killed. Britain – and Reading – suffer the worst storms in two hundred years. The Poll Tax is announced, adding to the housing problems facing many local people.*

October 1987 was a bad month for weather and an even worse one for weather forecasting. The first two weeks saw freak levels of rain. In the first fifteen days, 7 inches of rain fell, which equalled the record level for the entire month of October. Many rivers in the south of England broke their banks twice within six days. Then the night of 16 October 1987 saw the least successful piece of weather forecasting since Noah's next-door-neighbour spent his last days building a sun-lounger. Right up to that evening's weather forecast on the television, nothing untoward was predicted. But what followed was the worst storm in almost two hundred years.* Gusts of 93mph, recorded at Heathrow, were typical of conditions throughout the south. Seventeen people were killed; fifteen million trees were blown down and the damage was estimated variously at between £100 and £300 million.

Many thousands of people had their electricity and telephones cut off; Southern Region rail services were closed down entirely and Sevenoaks in Kent became Oneoak, as the other six trees from which it took its name were flattened. Scenes reminiscent of the Blitz were to be found in many parts of southern England and it was predicted that future generations of children would ask: 'What did you do in the Great Wind, Daddy?'

But some people in Reading saw it coming. The European Centre for Medium Range Weather Forecasting on the Shinfield Road had the most sophisticated weather forecasting computer in the world. A full four days before the event, they predicted exceptional weather conditions. The French authorities acted on their warning and, despite suffering even more

*The worst storm in recorded history in Britain took place on the night of 26/27 November 1703, when an estimated 8,000 people in southern England were killed.

Damage from the 1987 storm.

ferocious winds than ours (134 mph was recorded in Normandy), only four people were killed in France. But the Meteorological Office computer at Bracknell thought it knew better. It predicted that the storm would break over France (so that would be all right, then) and that the winds would be some 20 miles an hour slower than they actually were.

Berkshire and Reading took their full share of the battering:

The whole of Berkshire began the massive mopping-up process after a week of freak weather left a trail of destruction around the county. The hurricane force gales which hit the south of England ripped through homes and powerlines, and were followed by torrential rain and overnight flooding in many places.

At Sonning, the Thames burst its banks, flooding the French Horn Restaurant, and in Park Lane in Arborfield a 50 metre stretch of road was swamped with 6 inches of water. The hurricane winds brought down over 300 trees, left bare powerlines sparking in the rain and brought chaos to the roads and railway lines. Many parts of the country were without their electricity and telephone services. Nine major roads were blocked. Near Reading, the Shinfield and Burghfield Roads were impassable due to fallen trees and flooding.

Emergency services were inundated by calls from anxious residents and Council workers have gone flat out this week, dealing with problems. The Southern Electricity Board pulled out all the stops, working round the clock to restore power to 60,000 customers over the weekend. But despite drawing in workers from South Wales, the Midlands, Swindon and Oxford, it was midweek before the last 3,000 customers had electricity restored.

One of the many victims of the record gusts and lashing rain were the Pallas family of Caversham Park Village. A 60-foot tree ripped through their roof, missing six-year-old Athinoulla and her parents Frixos and Eroulla by a few feet. 'I thought it was a bomb,' said Mr Pallas, from his next-door-neighbour's home in Queensway, Caversham Park Village. 'We were very lucky. I just grabbed my daughter and went next door. Firemen told us just to turn everything off and get out and not to come back. The house is unsafe.'

Branches poked through the bedroom roofs, rubble littered the landing and a four foot crack has appeared in a wall.

Two Tilehurst families had a lucky escape, too, when a thirty-footer toppled just inches from the front of their Hogarth Road homes. 'We were really lucky,' said Mr Brian Hadnam. 'It's just inches from the house. We had a real shock this morning when we opened the curtains.'

As with most disasters, there were vultures waiting to prey on others' misfortunes:

Conmen cash in on the storm
Cowboy contractors are cashing in on the damage left by last week's hurricane and conning pensioners out of huge sums of money.

With reputable firms facing a huge backlog of work in removing uprooted trees and repairing damaged roofs, tricksters are moving in with the elderly as their target. One insurance company spokesman revealed that an elderly person had been charged £300 for having just three tiles replaced. And a senior Thames Valley policeman issued a warning that he feared even more of the cowboys would try to make money out of the misfortune of the old. Detective Chief Constable Barry Rutherford said: 'They will milk the elderly for everything they are worth.'

The local authorities also faced dire financial consequences:

Council bosses are bracing themselves for harsh cutbacks in their spending next year because of the bill from the storms. With the final cost yet to be worked out,

'An elderly person had been charged £300 for having just three tiles replaced'

Damage from the 1987 storm.

the bill locally for the damage is already running into hundreds of thousands of pounds. And Reading Borough Council leaders are claiming that the Government will profit from the storm damage. Chairman of the Council's Leisure Committee, Martin Salter, said that under the complex rules for local authority spending, the Council would be penalised for overspending when it set next year's rates.

Reading Borough Council already knows that next year's Transport Committee budget will be hit by at least £100,000 for damage to roads and pavements. The cost to the Leisure Services Department, which looks after the parks, has now topped £35,000. At least 300 trees were destroyed in the gales and another 500 suffered severe damage. Leisure Services officer Mike Preston said, 'I believe it will be the best part of a hundred years before Prospect Park looks like it did before last Thursday night.'

THE POLL TAX – FAIRER BY FAR?

Local government finance was a matter of more general interest than usual, since the Government was about to introduce the Poll Tax (or Community Charge, as it was known to its rapidly dwindling band of supporters). This provoked a lively correspondence in the newspapers at the time, with many of the writers questioning the fairness of a system that charged a millionaire and someone just above the poverty line the same amount. This prompted a letter from a Community Charge fan:

The Community Charge proposals will ensure that nearly everyone will have to pay something and have a stake in their Council's finances. . . . The new legislation cannot come too soon for the ratepayers of Reading, who are witnessing almost daily increases in local authority spending, supposedly for better services. Here are

A poll tax demonstrator with a sense of history.

just a few more positive facts relating to the Community Charge:

80% of single persons will be better off; 83% of one-parent families will be better off; 85% of single pensioners living alone will be better off . . . (etc.)

. . . Truly, a much fairer system.

The unhappy precedent for a flat-rate tax per head had been established in Britain somewhat earlier, by King Richard II, and it had led to the Peasants' Revolt of 1381. As we shall see, the British public, ever mindful of tradition, followed in similar vein in 1989 and 1990. The ungrateful wretches responded to all this fairness, not to mention being made so much better off, by rioting in the streets, eventually leading to the abolition of the tax and contributing to the downfall of Prime Minister Margaret Thatcher.

HOUSING COSTS IN CRISIS

Housing, or rather the lack and cost of it, was a major preoccupation of the day. A survey by the Halifax Building Society reported that Reading was now the most expensive urban area in the south-east in which to buy a semi-detached house. The average price was £74,800 and rising rapidly. (It had gone up by 23.5 per cent in the previous year across the south-east.) It was argued that this was affecting the whole of the housing market, as buyers were forced to trade down by spiralling prices. There were concerns that many house-buyers were over-committed and that even a 1 per cent increase in the mortgage rate could sink some of them.

Employers, for their part, found housing costs a major barrier to the recruitment of staff and even the rented sector was suffering serious cost increases.

1988 GLORY DAYS AT ELM PARK

A year of disasters – the Piper Alpha oil-rig, the Lockerbie jumbo jet and Edwina Currie's efforts to promote the egg industry. But for Reading Football Club it was their moment of Wembley glory. The Battle for Berkshire is joined and the County Council move into Shire Hall – for the time being.

When Reading beat Cardiff in February 1988, they got to the fifth round of the FA Cup for the first time in sixty-three years. Something few people remembered at the time was that it avenged an earlier defeat that robbed Reading Football Club of its greatest moment. In 1927 Reading FC had been just ninety minutes away from an FA Cup Final. In the course of

Happy fans with their Simod Cup Final tickets, while the rest queue, 1988.

their cup run, they had Elm Park's biggest-ever crowd, 33,042, for the fifth-round tie against Brentford. (By its final days, Elm Park's capacity had been reduced to around 12,000, for safety reasons.)

In the semi-final, they were drawn to play Cardiff on the neutral territory of Wolverhampton Wanderers' ground. Equally neutral was *The Times*, whose reporter felt that it was a rotten match, the only distinction being that Reading were lousier than Cardiff. Cardiff won 3–0, with Reading resigning themselves to defeat long before the end. Cardiff went on to face Arsenal in what was the London team's first ever Cup Final. (Cardiff had been to Wembley twice within three years.) Cardiff won 1–0, and so took the FA Cup out of England for the first and only time, while Reading had to wait until 1988 for their moment of glory at Wembley.

Reading struggled in the old Second Division during the 1987/88 season. The only form they appeared to be able to find was in cup matches, and even here their performances sometimes lacked finesse, according to the *Chronicle*'s man on the terraces. On their way to the semi-finals of the Simod Cup, they beat Queen's Park Rangers, Oxford United ('not a pretty match to watch'), Nottingham Forest and Bradford City (a match played in driving rain with 'plenty of endeavour but little in the way of skill').

In the semis, they had a home draw against the FA Cup holders, Coventry. This, at least, provided 'ninety minutes of pulsating soccer' in which 'Reading fought like tigers against the more skilful midlanders'. The match finished 1–1 after extra time, and went to a penalty shoot-out. In a few minutes of high drama, Reading came back from 2–0 down to win the penalty contest 4–3.

Reading were now in their first real final in their 117-year history. True, they had been in the finals of events like the London War Cup and the Southern Floodlit Cup, but these were low-key events, played on ordinary league grounds. Quite apart from the glamour of the occasion, there was

The triumphant (and relegated)
Reading team of 1988.

big money involved. Reading stood to get a share of the gate receipts (possibly £200,000), sponsorship from Simod (£60,000 for the winner, half that for the loser) plus the income from all the souvenir shirts, mugs and other merchandise that they could sell.

Their opponents in the final were First Division Luton, but the Reading fans rallied behind their team, outnumbering those from Luton by at least 3 to 1. Some 40,000 of them made the trip to Wembley, dominating the total crowd of 61,740. For those travelling to the match by car, the *Chronicle* provided a cut-out paper scarf to stick in the back window and, for those wishing to travel in an alcoholic haze, Nino's Wine Bar in Duke Street produced a special Simod cocktail. No details of its main ingredients were given, but embrocation would seem to be a reasonable bet.

Reading went into the Final next to bottom of the Second Division, and were forced to play with a makeshift forward line. Few, apart from their most enthusiastic fans, would have predicted the outcome of the game. As the *Chronicle* reporter put it:

Words are difficult to find to describe Reading's performance – dazzling, exciting, tremendous, magnificent, pulsating, exhilarating hardly fit the bill, it was fitting of more praise than that. . . .

The facts are simply that they [Luton] totally underestimated Reading and, when taking a 13th minute lead, probably thought that it was a case of by how many goals they would win. This proved fatal for, what Reading lack in skill, they more than make up for in endeavour and determination, as Luton learned to their cost.

Reading players display the Simod Cup at the Civic Offices, 1988.

Four goals, from Gilkes, Tait, Beavon and Smillie, gave Reading the match and the Cup by a margin of 4–1. Some of the Reading fans were still in shock as skipper Martin Hicks raised the cup. The Council's Leisure Committee Chairman and Reading FC supporter Martin Salter spoke for them: 'If someone had told me at the beginning of the season that Reading were going to score four goals at Wembley, I'd have told them to see a doctor.' Or, as a departing Luton fan was heard to remark: 'I've never seen anything so embarrassing in all my life.'

Reading returned home to a civic reception, where the talk was all about building a super stadium that would befit such a well-supported club. But, once the euphoria evaporated, they still had to deal with their dismal form in the league. This they failed to do and the team achieved the unenviable double of cup-winners and relegation to the old Third Division in the same season.

BUILDING IN OUR BACK YARD

The crowds at the Final were relatively well-behaved – there were only twenty-one arrests, of which ten were Reading fans. But another battle was being fought at this time, dubbed 'The Battle for Berkshire' by the media. Secretary of State for the Environment Nicholas Ridley had just decided that Berkshire would have to take an extra 7,000 houses over and above those being proposed by Berkshire County Council in their Structure Plan.

The local Councils, Berkshire MPs and eighty-five parishes had signed up to a campaign of opposition, orchestrated through the *Chronicle*. Their mailbags were bulging with letters of opposition (and just one from a resident who wrote – some said from a padded cell – in favour of more development).

The campaign attracted some expected supporters – writer and nearby resident John Mortimer was an established supporter of the Campaign for the Preservation of Rural England – and some unexpected ones. Few can have been more incongruous than the Henley Member of Parliament and former Secretary of State for the Environment, Michael Heseltine. He had previously earned a place in the demonology of Berkshire by imposing an extra 8,000 houses – christened 'Heseltown' – on the county during his reign at the ministry. But, of course, things had been different in 1981 – the demands of the economy had forced him to impose the extra housing. Now, as he put it in a letter to Ridley: 'There is a grave and growing anxiety in the south of England about the self-evident ravages of the countryside that the pace of development there is causing. . . . Berkshire is a crucially important area, one where pressure is intense. We know there is going to be development in areas like this.'

But Ridley was having none of this tree-hugging nonsense from his Honourable friend. In a press release he said:

Some new land has to be allocated for development in the south-east and I for one am not prepared to rule out all such development which is necessary to cater for legitimate housing needs. If I did, I would then be blamed, with some justification, for the consequent lack of reasonably priced housing to sons and daughters of local people and for rising levels of homelessness.

It is easy to point at the 'greed' of developers. But they only exist because they have customers. Housing is not a form of environmental pollution. It is about people and families, where they work and where they live.

1990 | POLL TAX AND THE CANAL

The unpopularity of the Poll Tax leads to civil disobedience throughout Britain – including Reading's streets and courts. The Kennet & Avon Canal reopens after a long period of dereliction and the Council kick up a stink about the Whitley Whiff.

The town's waterways have been central to its life ever since the days before William the Conqueror, when the Danes used to sail along them and drop anchor at Reading for a spot of looting and pillaging. In the Middle Ages, the Abbey and the Merchant Guild used to charge tolls on the boats that traded along the rivers. For many years, Reading was the westernmost point of navigation along the Kennet, and this drew much business into the town.

There was thus great concern when the Kennet Navigation Act was passed in 1715 and work began to make the river navigable as far as Newbury. Rioters, led by no less a person than the town's mayor, Robert Blake, tried unsuccessfully to destroy the works. Ironically, his name was later given to the first lock – Blake's Lock – on the Kennet & Avon Canal in Reading. Then, in 1794, Parliamentary approval was given for a new 55-mile stretch of canal linking Newbury to Bath and the River Avon, and creating a trade route between London and the port of Bristol. The canal finally opened in 1810.

It had enjoyed its supremacy for only thirty years when the Great Western Railway linked London and Bristol and rapidly began eroding the canal's trade. By 1852 the Great Western Railway had bought out the canal and, not surprisingly, did little to promote its use. They were, however,

Industries line the south bank of the Thames in 1936 – in the 1970s the Waterways Plan promoted their removal.

required by the Regulation of Railways Act to keep it in a navigable state, which they just barely did, up to the nationalisation of the railways in 1947. Those who expected things to improve thereafter were in for a disappointment, as the canal slipped steadily into disuse. By the 1950s protesters tried to paddle the length of it in canoes to publicise calls for its restoration, but even their tiny craft had to be carried for part of the way.

The turning point for the canal as a whole came with the formation of the Kennet & Avon Canal Trust in 1962. Almost thirty years of campaigning and hard work by them finally had its reward in August 1990, when the Queen went to Devizes to reopen the restored navigation. In the run-up to the reopening, Reading staged a Waterways Festival, with a theatre company based on a canal boat, dance, music and crafts and an armada of canal boats. Magicians, jugglers, Punch and Judy shows, clowns and someone from the museum displaying a history of the canal, completed the festivities.

Reading, too, had had its own long campaign to restore the setting of the waterways within its boundaries. For many years in the nineteenth and early twentieth centuries the town had turned its back on both the Thames and the Kennet. They served for a long time as Reading's sewers and many of the town's most noxious industries were located along their banks. Attempts were made to remedy this from the 1970s onwards, when the Council produced its first Waterways Plan, rather ambitiously described in the press at the time as the blueprint for turning Reading into 'a little

Canoeists bring news of the re-opening of the Kennet & Avon Canal, 1990.

Venice'. This was designed to guide the improvement of the rivers and their setting. In the succeeding years much of the unsightly riverside industry has given way to housing and more appropriate activities, and a continuous network of public footpaths is gradually being developed along their banks.

Within days of the reopening, the Mayor of Reading received another delegation of canoeists, greeting them on board the Council's own narrow boat *Reada*. This time, however, they were not carrying a petition to save the canal, but simply bearing greetings from the Mayor of Devizes to mark the fact that the canal was now fully operational. At the time, the canal was lucky to have any water at all for them to sail on, for this was the hottest and driest August on record. Hosepipes were banned and even the start of the local football leagues was pushed back to the end of September, to allow the pitches time to recover. The only gratuitous use of water was to be found at the Reading Rock Festival, where staff threw buckets of the stuff over the sweltering fans, to keep them cool, man.

NEAR DISASTER ON THE RAILWAY

Reading narrowly escaped a major rail disaster in August 1990. The incoming train from Tonbridge was supposed to go into platform 4B of the newly rebuilt station. Instead, it ploughed into the train on the next platform, waiting to leave for Waterloo. The roof of the train from Kent was said to have peeled back like an orange as the front coach embedded itself in the other train. Forty-one people were injured and rescue workers battled for hours to free some of them from the wreckage. One eye-witness described the crash as sounding as if a bomb had gone off, and it was generally agreed to be a miracle that nobody on the two packed trains was killed.

THE WHIFF GOES ON . . . AND ON . . .

The sewage works at Whitley, first established in 1875, were an important advance for the health of the town and, as we have seen, encouraged some

The scene at Reading's 1990 rail crash.

outlying areas to become incorporated into Reading. At first, the treatment of the sewage was very rudimentary indeed. It was simply spread out across the farmland there and left to decompose. The nuisance this method of treatment caused was not a great problem so long as the surrounding areas were undeveloped. But from the 1920s onwards Whitley started to become a residential area and the curse of the Whitley Whiff was born. The first record of complaint I found while researching this book dates from 1926. But

One of the rail crash victims is freed.

improvements in sewage treatment technology failed to solve the problem adequately and for years local residents and the Borough Council have fought battles with the operators to get less obnoxious treatment processes introduced.

A particularly bad case of what was thought to be the Whitley Whiff pervaded the whole town in August 1990. Cyclists reported feeling so ill from it that they had to dismount from their machines and rest – preferably without breathing. Office workers in the town centre (including – some felt with a kind of poetic justice – the Thames Water staff in Vastern Road) were forced to close all their windows. But for once, the sewage works were not to blame. No fault could be found at Smallmead and the problem was put down to farmers on the edge of the town spreading slurry on their land and failing to plough it in.

The Borough Council tried shaming Thames Water into doing something about the smell. They launched a Whitley Whiff Hotline and a door-to-door leaflet campaign, to find out the extent of the problem. They got over 500 replies to their leaflets, with three-quarters of respondents saying that they suffered from the nuisance and two-thirds claiming that their health was affected by it. The Council threatened to take Thames Water to court.

For their part Thames Water claimed that they had already spent £750,000 on trying to solve the problem and were sprinkling £20,000 worth of deodorant a year into the offending parts of the system. They had even brought in experts from Germany to advise them what to do. The problem was, it seemed, that the inconsiderate customers insisted on making regular use of their lavatories. This prevented Thames Water from taking the system out of commission entirely to do more comprehensive work on it. So, it was all our fault! If we would all just wait for a few weeks before going to the loo, all would be well!

The problem with the Whitley Whiff was, it seemed, that the inconsiderate customers insisted on making regular use of their lavatories

ANOTHER CRISIS AT ELM PARK

That August Reading Football Club had just signed its third new player in about a week, prompting the editorial column of the *Chronicle* to suggest that they should use some of their money instead to start providing a new stadium. A move away from the Dickensian conditions at Elm Park would, it was felt, benefit both players and supporters. (Interestingly, once the new stadium was under construction, the complaint was that they were too preoccupied with the premises, and should spend more money on new players.) Rather than buy in ready-made players at huge expense – something Reading Football Club is not often accused of doing – it was suggested that they should instead snap up some of the talent from the local youth teams. This was something the then current Chairman of Reading Football Club would have known about. Roger Smee had gone to the Forest School at Winnersh, and had been signed by Reading FC before going on to play for Chelsea and in Europe. The money he made from football enabled him to set up as a property developer, and his company, Rockfort, made him rich enough to become the Chairman of the club he had once played for.

But Roger Smee would not be able to help them pay for a new stadium. It was announced in that same month of August that shares in Rockfort – which had begun its stock market listing at 140p in 1988 – had slumped to 9p, and that dealing in the shares was suspended. Of equal concern to the town was that Rockfort was a partner in the Oracle development, a scheme that would one day transform the long-derelict Courage Brewery site into a major shopping and leisure centre. The Oracle project was delayed while some of Rockfort's development partners took over its share of the scheme.

In September Roger Smee announced that he was selling his near 30 per cent interest in the football club in order to spend more time with his ailing company. This meant that a majority shareholding in Reading FC was now up for sale, since a further 23 per cent share was already being marketed by that well-known philanthropist, Robert Maxwell. He had bought it some seven years before, with the idea of merging the club with

Police hold back crowds of happy residents, eager to pay their Poll Tax. Or possibly not, 1990.

Oxford United. The unspeakable mongrel offspring of this union was to have been called the Thames Valley Royals, and based in the wilds of Oxfordshire. After this idea sank without trace, Maxwell lost interest in the club, and he now wanted the cash to help him in his bid to buy Tottenham Hotspur.

Reading FC's financial problems paralleled those of their former Chairman. The entire playing staff were put on the transfer list, to see if there was any interest in any of them. There certainly wasn't much interest on the part of the fans. Attendances at Elm Park had slumped to 2,000–3,000, though the club blamed the poor attendances on the downturn in the economy – nothing whatsoever to do with the fact that Reading had lost eight out of their last nine games and were playing like donkeys.

AXE THE TAX!

The Poll Tax protests were at their height. When the Borough Council met in March to set the level of the tax, some five hundred protesters gathered outside the Civic Offices. Only twenty people – mostly journalists – were allowed into the Council Chamber and attempts to cool the rising anger of those left outside fell on deaf ears (if they were heard at all, above the shouting). Then some of the demonstrators tried to force their way in, through the line of police guarding the building. When five of their number were arrested, an estimated 150 of the demonstrators even tried to storm the police station and release their captured comrades.

Some of the demonstrators themselves were clearly terrified by this turn of events and claims were made later that the violence was started by outside extremists, brought in for the express purpose of causing trouble. This was vehemently denied by the organisers, but Councillor Tony Page was in no doubt: 'These people are Toy-Town Trots, bussed-in to cause mayhem and play on the genuine fear of the Tory Poll Tax. You see the same faces at all the meetings. They must be jet-lagged, the amount of travelling they do.'

Poll tax protestors – happy in their work, 1990.

Despite government forecasts that the Poll Tax rate would be below £300, Reading set a tax level of £447. The average for the whole of Berkshire was £420. Setting the tax proved to be the easy part, however. Collecting it was quite another matter. It was estimated that the collection costs alone would add £2–£3 million to the Council's expenses. By the middle of July Reading Borough Council issued 25,000 reminders to those who had not paid – about 25 per cent of all Poll Tax payers had not yet handed over a penny. It may have been just as well that the Council was not being bombarded with money, since the £2.2 million computer that the Council had bought in to process the payments kept breaking down.

The protesters, for their part, had plans – once the cases reached court – to clog up the legal system by persuading as many of the non-payers as possible to turn up at court in person. They were planning to send out 40,000 leaflets to encourage civil disobedience by the good citizens of Reading. The County Council, fearful of all this anarchy, used legislation originally designed to stop the National Front from using Council premises to ban Poll Tax protests from its buildings.

When the court hearings started in September, the protesters were true to their promise of causing chaos. A crowd of about 300 demonstrated outside the courts, shouting and waving banners. Inside, the courts eventually had to be cleared, as successive groups of demonstrators made noisy scenes. As the court struggled to get through its first 150 cases, defaulters, well briefed by the protest organisers, reduced the proceedings to a crawl by raising legal points and other delaying tactics.

These first few cases were just the tip of a very large iceberg. Reading Borough Council had court cases outstanding against some 9,000 defaulters. The secretary of the town's Anti-Poll Tax Coordinating Group, Dave Warren, warned that there could be violence if bailiffs were sent in to recover the money: 'I just don't know what would happen. If bailiffs are sent in, we will try to assist any communities which are trying to resist them. We would attempt to reason verbally with the bailiffs.'

Whenever the public were admitted to hear the cases being tried, the proceedings were reduced to the level of a pantomime by them cheering every point the accused scored and booing the authorities at every opportunity. One of the accused told the Bench: 'Well, I'm skint and it will be a toss-up whether the bailiffs get the goods or the bank gets the house on repossession.' As he left the court, he turned to the magistrate and added, 'I shouldn't leave it too long, mate.' Another, on having a liability order served on him, told the court, to cheers from his supporters 'Fair enough, it'll be the nick for me. I could do with a bit of porridge.'

By October the courts had got the machinery working again. Cases were going through in less than sixty seconds and some 1,100 protesters had had liability orders served on them, allowing the Council to send in the bailiffs. The Borough Council by then had raised £16 millions and were ahead of their target for collection. But the process did not always go according to plan. One case was dropped when it was discovered that the accused had received his summons two days before his first Poll Tax demand arrived!

But the protesters had not finished yet. Later that month, the court was emptied by a hoax bomb scare and further interruptions to proceedings meant that a hundred cases had to be adjourned for lack of time. Many cases of hardship were brought to the court's attention. In one case, a tearful former Japanese prisoner of war told the court how his erstwhile captors had reduced him to one meal a day, and that the demands of paying the Poll Tax were now doing the same to him. He was given the comforting advice: 'Your means or ability to pay is not a matter for the court.'

By now, the Council's machinery for collecting the Poll Tax was creaking badly again. They were being swamped by 1,100 telephone calls a week and innumerable visitors to the Civic Offices, trying to sort out their Poll Tax problems. Substantial backlogs were building up in the processing of payments, resulting in some entirely blameless individuals receiving summonses. By November 1990 an end to this chaos was in prospect. Margaret Thatcher had been removed as Prime Minister and the first priority for the new Environment Secretary – Henley MP Michael Heseltine – was to carry out a fundamental review of the Community Charge (as almost nobody now called it).

The Town Hall had by now been reprieved from demolition or sale, and work was in progress to refurbish it. Despite the best efforts of a drunken construction worker to burn it down (doing £250,000 of damage and earning himself two years in prison in the process), this first phase of the restoration won awards from the Civic Trust and the Royal Institute of British Architects.

BOTTOM BRICKED OVER

Another long-running saga came to a less happy solution, as far as many Reading people were concerned, in 1990. Developers had been trying to build on Bugs Bottom in Caversham virtually since the Second World War. Repeated attempts to gain planning permission had been thrown out on appeal but in 1984 house-builders Higgs & Hill tried again. This time the Secretary of State for the Environment Nicholas Ridley decided to allow the appeal – his decision was announced the day after a General Election – and a long process of challenging his decision in the courts followed.

By 1990 the conventional legal processes were exhausted and the protesters turned to direct action. A large hoarding on wheels was pushed by protesters – some of them dressed as giant rabbits – from Reading to the House of Commons, where a petition bearing 17,000 signatures was

'Your means or ability to pay is not a matter for the court'

Bug's Bottom protestors, dressed for the press, 1990.

*The Bug's Bottom poster pull
protest failed to save the valley.*

handed in. There was an attempt to use the 1832 Caversham Enclosure Act to argue that development could not take place in the area. (One potential downside to this, had it been upheld in the courts, might have been that all the other housing built in the area since 1832 would also be illegal and should, strictly speaking, be demolished.) The protesters even had their own television programme about their campaign. But none of it was to any avail, and during the 1990s the valley gradually turned from farmland to housing estate.

1999 AND BEYOND

THE FUTURE FOR READING

The nation prepares for a new millennium, as Reading Football Club play their first season in their new home and the Oracle is about to transform Reading town centre.

After the closure of the Courage Brewery, there was a predictable battle over the future of this key town centre site. It ended, after a planning inquiry in 1980, with most of the area to the west of Bridge Street designated for housing and the area to the east to provide yet another large-scale office development. Reading was at this time under siege by office developers. In a single year during the 1980s, the Council's planning department dealt with applications for around 1.2 million square feet of office development – enough to increase the town's already considerable stock of offices by roughly a quarter.

The housing part of the site was soon built, but the office part stood derelict throughout the 1980s. It was in 1989 that the idea of a shopping development on the site began to emerge, and was given the name of the Oracle. The name derived from a charitable institution built on part of the same site in 1627–8 as the result of a bequest from a wealthy Reading-born clothier, John Kendrick. Its original purpose was to provide a workhouse to employ the poor of Reading in the clothing trade. The name 'Oracle' is variously thought to come from the word for a response to an

THE FUTURE FOR READING

appeal from God, a corruption of the words 'work hall', the Italian clothing dye 'oricello', or the word for a porch or entrance, 'oriolum'. The workhouse was eventually demolished in 1850.

The Oracle shopping centre was another Reading scheme with a long gestation period. It suffered from the ups and downs of the economic cycle and, with it, the changing fortunes of its would-be developers. (We heard earlier about the demise of one of the development partners, Rockfort.) Another of its problems was finding a suitably prominent front door on to the town's prime shopping street, Broad Street. The original scheme took its access from Minster Street, but investors were not convinced that this was a strong enough link to the town centre. It was only when Debenhams' department store was brought into the scheme and their Broad Street frontage became the entrance to the new development that investors were persuaded of the scheme's viability.

The new development, which is currently (1999) under construction will increase the size of the town's shopping centre by one-third and put Reading among the top twenty shopping centres in the country. It will add to the choice of leisure in the town centre, with a multiplex cinema, a crèche and assorted eating and drinking places. Open areas along the banks of the Kennet will provide a focal point for the performing arts – unspecified 'vibrant activities' are promised, where once Simonds' Brewery loaded its products and bargees struggled to navigate their craft through the dangerous and narrow part of the waterway known as the Brewery

The Reading Half-Marathon – part of the town's sporting calendar for many years.

Edward Heath rehearses Reading's Arion Orchestra for a concert, 1980.

Gut. A total of 2,500 multi-storey car parking places will be provided, dwarfing the car park at Chatham Street – though it is unlikely that users of the new scheme will be allowed a week of free parking to get used to the unfamiliar concept of parking indoors, as they were with Chatham Street in 1968.

FIELD OF DREAMS

For over a century, the home of Reading Football Club was a 4-acre former gravel pit, which they originally leased for the princely sum of £100 per year. They played their first match at Elm Park in September 1896 against a team from Holloway College in London, appearing under the memorable title of 'Mr A. Royston Bourke's London XI'. The local MP, Mr C.T. Murdoch, and the Mayor of Reading were present to open the stadium, in front of a crowd of 2,500.

Mr Murdoch declared the ground to be 'second to none in the Kingdom'. It had cost them £800 to lay out and fence the pitch and another £500 for the grandstand and other buildings (compared with the estimated £37 million for the new stadium). The team did not have the most auspicious start at their new home. Reading completely outclassed their opponents and had built up a lead of 7–1, before a thunderstorm flooded the pitch and forced the abandonment of the game. To add to the débâcle, the Football Association later fined Reading £5 for playing against a team not registered with the FA.

Students of inflation may care to note that admission in those days was sixpence. Boys and, for some reason, ladies got in for half price. (The possibility of female children attending appeared not to have occurred to the management.) Admission to the enclosure was three pence extra and the services of the Reading Temperance Prize Band were thrown in at no extra cost. Temperance was the order of the day generally in those early years, since one of the conditions of the lease of the land was that no betting or sale of alcoholic beverages should take place there.

The playing surface was not as perfect as Mr Murdoch suggested. The flooding that wiped out the first match proved to be a more perennial problem. Elm Park had a serious tendency to flood and nine attempts were made in the following thirty years to solve it. More recently, in 1986, ruts in the pitch had to be ironed out with the aid of a steamroller to enable a match to take place.

Reading FC joined the Football League in 1920. In addition to Reading's cup and league matches, the ground has also hosted a variety of other events, including an FA Cup semi-final replay, a schoolboy international (1911–12), a cricket Test Match (1902) and the Amateur Cup Final (1913–14). World heavyweight boxing champion Joe Louis fought there as a US serviceman in the Second World War. It was also the setting for a 1988 television series about a football team, *The Manageress*, in which a number of Reading players and supporters appeared as extras. But perhaps the most famous real player to put on a Reading shirt was former Manchester United star George Best, who played for the team in a friendly against New Zealand in 1984. United's famous manager, Matt Busby, also had strong links with Reading, playing with the club throughout the war years.

Despite the lavish expenditure on the ground in 1896, further improvements were eventually needed. In 1946 a public address system was introduced. Prior to that, the scores in other key games were relayed to the ground via the *Chronicle* offices and paraded around the touchline by a boy with a blackboard. Floodlights arrived in 1954 and were first used in a friendly against Racing Club de Paris. There were fears that the inclusion of night-time matches would tempt the club to play too many games and thus weaken their players' stamina. In 1956 the pampered fans even had the railway sleepers that made up the terracing at the two ends removed, and replaced with concrete terracing and crush barriers.

On the debit side, the West Stand blew down in a storm in 1925 and was never rebuilt. And £50,000 had to be spent in 1980 on segregation fences

The proposed view along Riverside from the new bridge facing the cinema complex, Debenhams and car parking.

to try to stem the rising tide of soccer hooliganism. But soccer terrorism was not solely the prerogative of the young. During the 1970/1 season, one of the visiting team's players was bending down to pick the ball out of the net when an elderly spectator leapt over the fence and stabbed him in the bottom with an umbrella! But perhaps the oddest case of hooliganism occurred in 1927, during the match in which Reading won a fifth-round FA Cup tie in front of their biggest ever crowd. One of the Reading supporters was accompanied by a dog, dressed in the club colours. It bit one of the opposing supporters, leading to its owner being fined.

Many of the club's highest and lowest points have been acted out at Elm Park. Reading achieved their highest ever score there in 1946 when they won 10–2 against Crystal Palace in a Division Three (South) match. They very nearly knocked Manchester United out of the FA Cup in 1955. United snatched a very late equaliser, when even their manager Matt Busby had given up the game for lost, and then went on to beat Reading 4–1 in the replay at Old Trafford. And it was on their home ground that Reading won their way through to the final of the Simod Cup in 1988. At the other extreme, the lowest crowd ever to watch a league game at Reading was 1,713, who turned up for a match against Preston North End in 1982. During the great freeze of 1947 the ice on the pitch had to be broken with a pickaxe before the match could take place, and the visiting goalkeeper faced the additional distraction of being snowballed.

Despite its historic associations Elm Park was not up to modern standards by the 1990s and its location in a densely built-up area made it a nuisance to many of its neighbours. After many years of debate, a site and – no less important, the £37 million finance – was found to build the new 25,000 all-seater Madejski stadium in the Smallmead area of south Reading. The team played its last league match at Elm Park in May 1998 against Norwich. Not for the first time in their history, Reading FC managed to turn what should have been a celebration into a wake. They

The television series 'The Manageress' is filmed at Elm Park, 1988.

were relegated that season, and their last league game at Elm Park was also their last (one hopes only for the time being) in the First Division.

The first game at the Madejski Stadium in August 1998 was in marked contrast to the opening of Elm Park. For one thing the crowds in 1896 would have been more than a little surprised to see parachutists jumping from an aeroplane and landing on the pitch. They might also have marvelled at the food on offer in the executive suites: terrine of guinea fowl, glazed fillet of wild salmon and lobster mayonnaise dressed in prawn tails. Whatever happened to the people's game? However, those in the stands were still subsisting on hot dogs and coke, and there was still a marching band at half time.

Outside the ground afterwards there were no trams, just the biggest car park in league football and mammoth traffic jams as the 18,000 spectators crawled home past the uncompleted A33 relief road that would eventually serve the ground. Best of all, the team managed to have a sense of occasion for once. They beat Luton – coincidentally their opponents in the 1988 Simod Cup Final – by 3–0.

WHATEVER NEXT?   2000

The final pages of this book are being written in the autumn of 1998. As I write, the town seems to have much to look forward to in the new century. The town centre has already benefited greatly from town centre management and pedestrianisation, and the Oracle should lift it into a new league as a shopping centre. From being a deserted and sometimes threatening place outside normal working hours, the town centre has also begun to develop a night-time leisure economy that draws in people from a wide area. The Oracle and the completion of the Town Hall refurbishment will add to the range of leisure attractions Reading is able to offer. Outside the town centre, there are regeneration projects to help breathe new life into areas such as the Oxford Road that have suffered relative decline and deprivation over the years.

Fifty years of peace and relative prosperity have given the town low unemployment and there is a lot of highly paid work in growth industries. But there are still plenty of challenges for the town. Housing has been a perennial problem throughout the century and current forecasts point to a dramatic increase in the numbers of households in the area into the new millennium. The affordability of housing is likely to remain a problem in an area of high house prices.

The motor car, which originally seemed to be a force for liberation, now has the potential to choke Reading with noise, pollution and congestion. Ambitious plans exist to tackle the problem but, given the present rate of funding from central government, my successor, chronicling the approach of the 22nd century, may still be looking forward to the completion of the current programme. What is needed is some innovative form of public transport – something using non-polluting, quiet, renewable sources of energy. Something like . . . horse trams, perhaps?

INDEX

Arion Orchestra 120
Aviation:
　balloning 16
　parachuting 53–4
　Reading airfield 52–4

Brewery: Simonds/Courages: 23, 25,
　40, 100–1, 118
Buffalo Bill 8

Car parks 77–8
Caversham:
　boundary extension 12–16
　bridge 42, 45
　Park Village 89–90
Cinemas 14, 26, 61, 95
Civil disorder:
　Anti-Thatcher 102
　Boer War 3
　Poll tax 115–17
Coop Jam Factory 58–9, 78
Cricket:
　A.P.F. Howard 46

Decimal coinage 73

Education 5, 71
Elections 39
Emmer Green caves 93–4

Fascism and Hitler 46–9
Floods 61–7
Football:
　Reading FC 4, 11, 24, 102, 106–9,
　　114–15, 120–3

Gas lighting 6–7, 16

Heseltine, Michael MP 86, 110, 117
Housing 37–8, 106, 109–10

Bugs Bottom 117–18
Hunger marchers 49–50
Huntley & Palmer 18, 22, 24, 30,
　38–9, 44, 45, 91–2

Immigration and racism 70–3
Influenza 34, 36–7

Kool Kat Club 67–8

Lower Earley 96

Maxwell, Robert 114–15
Medicines, patent 3–4
Mikardo, Ian MP 63
Motoring 5, 12, 16

Palace Theatre 69–70
Parks:
　Caversham Court 52
　Prospect 7
　Thameside Promenade 15
Police 82–3, 92–3
Poll tax 105–6, 115–17
Pop music:
　Punk 94–5
　Rock Festival 79–84
Powell, Enoch 72, 73

Railway accident 112
Reading Borough Council 37, 69–70,
　84–5, 85–6, 96–8, 104–5
　Day, Jim 99
　Hexagon 90–1
　Page, Tony 99, 115
　Salter, Martin 105, 109
　Sutton, Edith 50–1
Reading Bridge House 70
Reading Chronicle 1, 2, 7, 8, 10–11,
　12, 15, 22, 28, 30, 32, 33–4, 39,

50, 51, 56, 63–5, 72, 73, 77, 79,
　81, 84, 107, 108, 109, 121
Rivers and canals 19, 32, 55–6, 110–12
Royalty:
　Coronation 17–18
　Silver Jubilee 96
　visits 44–5, 92–3

Shopping:
　Broad Street Mall 74–6, 85
　Oracle 118–20
　Self-service 73
　Supermarkets 74
Smee, Roger 114
Storms 103–5
Strike, General 39–44
Suffragettes 16–17
Suttons Seeds 24, 25, 45, 87–8

Telephones 51
Tilehurst 6
Town planning 51–2, 84–5
Traffic 76–8
　A329(M) motorway 88–9
　Inner Distribution Road 98–9
　M4 motorway 86–7
Trams 8–11, 27, 40–2, 56–7
Trolley buses 54–5, 77

University 18, 67

Wars:
　Boer 1–2
　First World 19–36
　Second World 56–61
Welfare 5–6
Whitley Whiff 45–6, 112–14
Wilson, Leslie MP 21

X, Malcolm 73